GREEN DOG, GOOD DOG

GREEN DOG, GOOD DOG

Reducing Your Best Friend's Carbon Paw Print

Dominique De Vito

With Dr. Robert Goldstein, VMD, and Susan Goldstein,
Directors of the Healing Center for Animals and Earth Animal

LARK BOOKS

A Division of Sterling Publishing Co., Inc.
New York / London

SENIOR EDITOR Deborah Morgenthal   ART DIRECTOR Amy Sly
ILLUSTRATOR Susan McBride   COVER DESIGNER Amy Sly

Library of Congress Cataloging-in-Publication Data

De Vito, Dominique.
  Green dog, good dog : reducing your best friend's carbon paw print /
Dominique C. De Vito, with Robert Golstein and Susan Goldstein. -- 1st ed.
     p. cm.
  Includes index.
  ISBN 978-1-60059-350-5 (pb-trade pbk. : alk. paper)
  1. Dogs--Environmental aspects. 2. Environmental protection--Citizen
participation. I. Goldstein, Robert S., 1942- II. Goldstein, Susan, 1947-
III. Title.
  SF427.D37 2009
  636.7--dc22
                                    20080454

10 9 8 7 6 5 4 3 2 1

First Edition

Published by Lark Books, A Division of
Sterling Publishing Co., Inc.
387 Park Avenue South, New York, NY 10016

Text © 2009, Lark Books
Illustrations © 2009, Susan McBride

Distributed in Canada by Sterling Publishing,
c/o Canadian Manda Group, 165 Dufferin Stree
Toronto, Ontario, Canada M6K 3H6

Distributed in the United Kingdom by GMC Distribution Services,
Castle Place, 166 High Street, Lewes, East Sussex, England BN7 1XU

Distributed in Australia by Capricorn Link (Australia) Pty Ltd.,
P.O. Box 704, Windsor, NSW 2756 Australia

Every effort has been made to ensure that all the information in this book is accurate. However, due to
differing conditions, tools, and individual skills, the publisher cannot be responsible for any injuries, losses,
and other damages that may result from the use of the information in this book.

If you have questions or comments about this book, please contact:
Lark Books
67 Broadway
Asheville, NC 28801
828-253-0467

Manufactured in China

This book was printed on recycled paper with agri-based inks.

ISBN 13: 978-1-60059-350-5

For information about custom editions, special sales, premium and corporate purchases, please contact
Sterling Special Sales Department at 800-805-5489 or specialsales@sterlingpub.com.

Dedication

For Chief and Cinderella first and foremost, the Dalmatians who are my inspiration, my motivation, and the beneficiaries of what I hope is a much cleaner, greener, healthier, and longer life through the research I did for this book.

For Dawson and Dylan, my sons. May their future and that of their generation be one we can all be proud of, starting today.

And for my husband, Carlo. By bringing us back to the earth, you may not have made life easier for us, but you certainly made it more meaningful, and for that I am especially grateful. There is perspective on the knoll above the vineyard.

I love you all, with all my heart and soul.

Acknowledgments

I could not have written this book without the profound lessons I've learned from Dr. Bob and Susan Goldstein—not just in the years that I've known them, but in the feedback they gave as consultants to the text itself. Their professional accolades are many—on the veterinary and business sides—but it is their sincere empathy for the well-being of all animals that truly sets them apart. They were pioneers in looking for healthier alternatives for companion animals, and have made it possible for so many to spend extra time with their beloved animal friends. Theirs is a special gift they bring to this world, and I am so blessed to know them.

Speaking of special, I have to thank Deborah Morgenthal, Senior Editor for Lark Books and my coach and friend during the writing of this book. Your advice was always spot on, and most appreciated. Thank you!! Susan Huxley was an exceptional copy editor, and Amy Sly brought the book together with a terrific design.

David Frei, Director of Communications for the Westminster Kennel Club, was especially generous with his time and perspective on purebred dogs.

On a larger scale, we wouldn't be having this conversation if it weren't for the tireless efforts of truly dedicated folks to make going green a part of our everyday vocabulary for the 21st century—and beyond.

CONTENTS

Dedication 5
Acknowledgments 5
Introduction 8

1 Greening the Feeding of Your Dog 12
- How to make sense of commercial pet foods
- Options for greener feeding
- Choices that are good for your dog and the planet

2 Greening the Health of Your Dog 30
- What green healthcare means for you and your dog
- How to find and work with a green veterinarian
- Holistic approaches to greening your dog for a lifetime

3 Greening Your Dog House— That's *Your* House! 68
- How to do an overall home assessment
- Options for green cleaning
- How to make greener choices for your dog—and yourself

4 Greening Your Yard 90
- How to do an overall yard assessment
- How to start greening your yard for your dog
- How to maintain a dog-friendly & eco-friendly yard

5 Doo-ing the Green Thing   108

- Why picking up after your dog is so important
- Options for greener waste maintenance
- How to green-up after your dog

6 Greening the Goods of Your Dog   118

- How to provide your dog with green supplies
- Ways to apply the reduce, reuse, recycle mantra to the things in your dog's life
- How to cultivate a less = more attitude

7 Greener Getaways with Your Dog   136

- What it means to travel green
- How to cope when life takes you and your dog beyond local
- How to be green in other places

8 Deep Greening Your Dog   154

- What to do to make the ultimate green start
- Ways to get green-centives
- How to remember that today is tomorrow

Resources 168
Index 176

Good for Your Dog, Good for the Planet

If, like millions of people, you're concerned about the global climate crisis and the wastefulness culture that seems to be engulfing us, and you've found yourself wanting to live more lightly on the earth...and you have a dog (or dogs)...welcome to the Green Dog community.

It may feel a bit radical or even indulgent to pick up a book about going green with your dog. (And isn't a lot of paper used in the production of books? We did use 30-percent post-consumer recycled paper and agri-based inks.) After all, aren't there more pressing issues to spend time on? Shouldn't you be helping out more in your kids' school or getting involved in local politics or community service?

Yes, there are always other important issues that need our attention. But consider this: while we canine caretakers have a very personal relationship with our four-footed friends that can feel very private, we are also a very large and influential demographic group. In the United States alone, it's estimated that there are more than 70 million dogs in over 40 million households. If even 10 percent of those households considered greener options for their dogs, we'd be talking 4 million households generating less electricity, opting for disposable waste bags, feeding diets supported by local ingredients, and doing many other things that support cleaner and greener living (and, by the way, better health for your pooch).

Think about it: do you walk your dog in areas where you need to pick up after him? If so, how do you

manage the waste? What are the effects of highly processed foods on our dogs and on the environment? What kind of home and yard are you providing for your dog—one that's maintained with biodegradable products, or with harsh chemicals? Do you know what's in the shampoo your dog groomer uses?

Carbon Paw Print 101

The way you live your life—and the way you care for your dog—constitute your dog's "carbon paw print," because they involve the resources you use for his health and well-being. A carbon footprint or paw print is nothing more than the sum of the services and products we use on a daily basis that are fossil-fuel (or carbon) based. Driving a car, using petroleum-based products, tapping into an electric grid, eating foods that require extensive shipping or produce harmful waste products—all these are examples. You can even approach reducing your own footprint via reducing your dog's paw print, because his is so greatly influenced by yours.

OUR LOVE KNOWS NO BOUNDS

The pet industry in the United States is huge — spending is approaching $50 billion annually, according to the American Pet Products Manufacturers Association (APPMA). The greatest percent of spending goes toward mass-produced foods (including treats) at $16 billion, with veterinary care and supplies/OTC medications ranking a distant (but significant) second ($10 billion) and third ($10 billion) respectively. The APPMA reports that industry trends for American dogs include more luxury items and services, increased travel, and of course, a larger variety of foods.

I'm part of the dog-loving world, and I wouldn't want it any other way. I can't imagine life without a dog or dogs, and I fret over mine with an almost irrational concern that my "human" family often finds irritating (I probably would, too). I'm lucky that they're nearly as nuts about our dogs as I am. I needed them to be when this project came along!

My Dog Résumé

I've had the great fortune to be involved in the dog-publishing world for several decades now, and as my career evolved, so did my thinking about all aspects of dog care. That's how it works for anyone who's passionate about something, and being passionate about dogs is easy. During these years I've been gratified to see dog-training books turn their focus from punishment-based to reward-based training; recommended diets evolve from completely processed to meaty bone-based ones; and healthcare expand from an annual check-up and booster shot to encompass not just a variety of alternative approaches, but a re-evaluation of the all-in-one shot itself. What progress! What a plethora of information sources and expertise we dog owners have to choose from!

Choosing Green

Some of the newest and most exciting dog care developments are the green care options and actions that are not only great for our dogs, but also help us, our families, our communities, our world, and our planet. That's what this book is all about. While this approach might feel awkward at first—just as it did to teach your dog to sit using a treat, instead of pulling his head up and pushing his bottom down—once you start changing, you'll recognize how much it's for the better. I thought I knew a lot about dogs and was making great choices for them based on my years in the "dog world." But I had no idea that area rugs and carpets were laden with chemicals with the potential to do so much harm to the dogs that innocently lie on them (not to mention our kids!). I hadn't considered that the plastic bags I was using to help keep the sidewalks in my neighborhood clean were contributing to major waste problems in landfills, where they become non-dissolving poop pellets (like disposable diapers). I didn't want to believe that the pet food recall of 2007 was, as Dr. Bob Goldstein succinctly stated, a pet food "wake-up call" that prompted many to change—not just the way their companion animals eat—but how we eat as well. The wake-up call woke me up, and I wrote this book to share what I've experienced and learned.

Making changes can be exciting and invigorating, but it can be scary and discouraging, too. It can feel as if you're failing, as if things aren't happening fast enough, and as if your efforts are in vain. This is the nature of change. The great thing about this book is that it shows you how you can make, in all the different areas of your life with your dog, simple changes that could significantly and positively affect your community and our planet. When you see how easy it is to adopt some of these changes and start incorporating them into your daily life, you'll wonder why you waited until now to go green with your dog. Plus, once you start down the green path with Fido, you'll soon be making greener choices in the rest of your life, too.

How to Use This Book

Using this book is easy: you can start at the beginning, or skip to the chapters that interest you most. Whether the topic is feeding or traveling with your dog, each chapter wraps up with an action plan that is organized by four levels of involvement. They are:

Level 1 - You're making a conscious choice to do something different for your dog.

Level 2 - You're making a strong effort to make a difference for your dog.

Level 3 - Your dog is living about as greenly as possible.

Level 4 - Your dog is so green that Al Gore should put her in his next slide show!

The four levels are provided so that change can happen for you gradually or more rapidly. As you move through them, I know you'll discover other devoted dog owners who share your views. More and more industries are addressing the issues that you'll be impacting, which makes getting and staying involved easier and more enjoyable. From food and health concerns to supplies, accessories, travel, and more, there's a lot to learn, and a lot to do. You can start right now. Your dog will thank you.

"It does not matter how slowly you go, as long as you don't stop."
—Confucius (551–479 B.C.)

Greening
THE
Feeding
OF YOUR
Dog

IN THIS CHAPTER YOU'LL LEARN

How to make sense of commercial pet foods

Options for greener feeding

Choices that are good for your dog and the planet

IN MY HOUSE, DOGGY DIN-DIN TIMES ARE DEFINITELY THE MOST EXCITING PARTS OF THE DAY FOR MY TWO DALMATIANS, CHIEF AND CINDERELLA. They are fed at around 6 AM and 3 PM. At both times you'd think these pampered pooches had never been fed before. They dance, they bark, and their eyes shine as they follow me from fridge to sink. If I'm putting something especially tasty in their bowls, they stand riveted, waiting. If I take too long, Chief starts to groan and Cinder gives her unique "whoo whoo" bark. Every day, twice a day, they meet their bowls with devotion, devour their food, check each other's bowls for remnants, lick their chops, and look at me to see if there's anything else. They are always disappointed that there's not.

This simple ritual of preparing meals for such expressive, happy animals replenishes me, too. While they're getting a meal, I'm being adored. My dogs make me feel good about providing their sustenance. They inspire me to make every doggy din-din interesting…special. But besides being such upbeat occasions in my day, doggy din-dins have effects that extend way past the few minutes it takes my dogs to eat. Those effects have to do with how healthy they are—and stay—and how their meals come to them through today's commercial processes (or not). If you want your dogs to live more lightly on this planet, looking at the "food chain" for them is a good way to start.

The Key Issues

Let's review some key questions related to feeding our dogs—questions that will help define the process and simplify decision-making relative to feeding greener. These include:

1. What is the food made with? What are its ingredients?
2. Does it need to be supplemented, and if so, with what?
3. What kind of packaging does it come in?
4. How much of it needs to be fed per meal?
5. What about treats—does my dog get a lot of them, and what kind are they?
6. What kinds of bowls are used for food and water? (See page 122.)
7. Does my dog seem to produce a lot of waste from what he eats? (See chapter 5.)

What's in the Food?

A good question that we don't often ask ourselves is, "What is our dog's food made with (and from)?" The mass production of dog food started less than 150 years ago, when American James Spratt decided there had to be a more convenient—and nutritious—source of food for dogs than some ship's biscuits he came across in his travels. He created a dough of ground vegetables and grains suitable for dogs, formed it into small pieces, and baked it. Spratt's Dog Cakes were born. This spawned the dog food industry, and today there are thousands of brands on the market. With all of them claiming to meet a dog's nutritional needs, how are we supposed to decide which one is best for our pooch, much less what type of "dog food" can benefit the planet? Read on!

Healthy = Green!

Like us, dogs are what they eat, and in a nutshell, if they are fed junk, their health will be junky. On the other hand, if they're fed foods that satisfy their nutritional requirements, they will exude good health. A healthy dog requires fewer care products and services—ranging from grooming supplies (shampoos, tear removers, ear cleaners, etc.) and pest control (flea and tick preventives) to medicines. And fewer products mean less waste of resources…which is a big part of going green!

The commercial dog food dilemma is a longstanding concern of the husband-and-wife team of Dr. Robert Goldstein and Susan Goldstein. (Dr. Bob, as he is known, is a graduate of the University of Pennsylvania veterinary school, and Susan is a passionate nutritionist and healer.) After 30 years of experience with animal health and nutrition, when so many ill dogs in their practice responded to simple nutritional supplements, they began to suspect the health claims that commercial food manufacturers were making. Here are some of the disclosures from their book, *The Goldsteins' Wellness & Longevity Program: Natural Care for Dogs and Cats*:

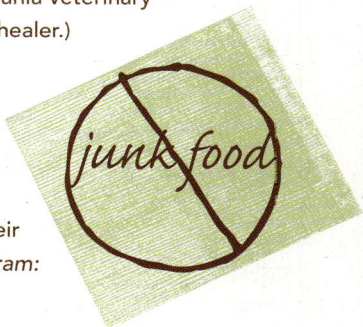

- To kill bacteria and extend shelf life, most pet food is cooked at very high temperatures. This also kills the live enzymes that are of nutritional value.
- Protein sources in commercial foods are often by-products that have been rejected for human consumption, such as feathers, beaks, cartilage, lungs, and so on.
- Grain sources are typically wheat, corn, and soybeans, which are often genetically engineered crops, or are grown with chemical fertilizers and sprayed with pesticides.

Be a Label Detective

If you want to know what's in your dog's food—whether it be in kibble or canned form—look past the pretty pictures and claims of improved health on the package, and go straight to the ingredients list. By law, any commercially available pet food must list all the ingredients in the product by their weight. For dogs, high-quality animal proteins should be at the top of the list. Obviously meat weighs more than a dried substance, but if the first ingredient is chicken, for example, and the second is chicken meal, you know that together they amount to a healthy dose of animal protein.

Here's what you want to see on the label:

A whole source of animal protein. This should be at—or near—the top of the ingredients list. For example, look for chicken followed by chicken meal (the meat itself has much of its water weight cooked out of it, which is why the meal is added—it's the dehydrated form of the protein). Organic is preferable.

Whole grains (preferably organic). Beware, though. When similar grains or grain by-products make up the first several listed ingredients, while they might not be contributing much individually, when added together, they may be a significant portion of the product—even outweighing the meat.

Omega fatty acids. These come from sources such as fish, flax, sesame, or sunflower.

Natural additives and preservatives. You'll see ingredients such as vitamin C or rosemary.

Beneficial minerals. These may be zinc proteinate or copper amino chelate.

BST-free. Labels on foods that are not genetically modified will indicate that they're BST-free.

UNDESIRABLE DOG FOOD INGREDIENTS

If you see a lot of the following ingredients on the label of your dog's food, you should reconsider your brand, as these provide little or no nutritional value and are primarily fillers or preservatives.

• Meat or poultry by-products

• By-product meals, including corn gluten meal and any unidentifiable meals such as "meat meal"

• Grain by-products such as middlings or bakery fines

• Processed grains like brewer's rice or wheat flour

• Saturated or highly saturated fats, or unsaturated vegetable oils

• Fillers or nonbeneficial materials like beet pulp or animal digest

• Inorganic sulfates and/or oxides such as zinc or iron oxide, or zinc proteinate

• Artificial preservatives like BHA, BHT, and ethoxyquin

• Additives, including colors, flavors, and—especially—sweeteners

If you're not sure about an ingredient, write it down and research it. Call the manufacturer for details, or ask your veterinarian. A great source of information is the *Whole Dog Journal* newsletter's annual dry dog food report. It's available through their website at whole-dog-journal.com.

While finding a whole source of animal protein at the top of your dog food's ingredients label may feel like a small victory on the way to feeding him better, it raises its own concern: Where did the

meat come from? Even human-grade meat is often factory farmed, and "livestock production generates nearly a fifth of the world's greenhouse gases—more than transportation," according to the Food and Agriculture Organization of the United Nations. This was reported in an article by Mark Bittman in *The New York Times* ("Rethinking the Meat Guzzler," January 27, 2008).

What's a Carnivore to Do?

With so many concerns about meat production, is the answer to turn our dogs into vegetarians? Veterinarians and animal nutritionists agree that it is not; in fact, animal protein and fat are the keys to a nutritious diet for dogs (and cats). The solution is simple: if you want to be green when it comes to what you feed your dog (and yourself!), opt for meats that are certified organic, or consider cooking your dog's food with cuts from locally raised livestock. To find a source near you, go to eatwellguide.org, and enter your zip or postal code.

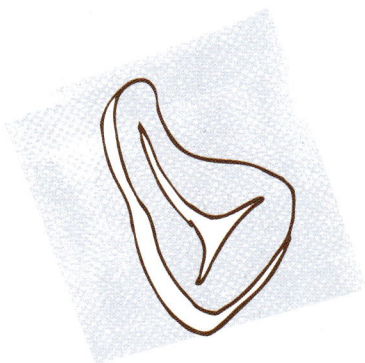

That's what Jessica Disbrow Talley and her husband, Eric Talley, did. The founders of the Bubba Rose Biscuit Company (offering homemade, all-organic, grain-free dog biscuits) are on the front lines of feeding dogs every day—theirs and others. While they themselves are vegetarians, they know meat is important for dogs, and they have been feeding their three dogs a raw-based diet (explained on page 24) for years. They started their business in response to the increasing interest of other dog owners in high-quality, human-grade (and local) ingredients. When the pet food recall of tainted products occurred in the spring and summer of 2007, interest surged—and has held steady.

Jessica believes there is a link between quality ingredients and a dog's health.

She explains: "The benefits are immediately apparent. When we began the company, I consulted with an unofficial dog nutritionist—a breeder and dog trainer who has been feeding all her show dogs a raw diet for 14 years now. Besides shedding light on some very common dog allergies—to wheat, corn, and soy—she opened my eyes to the world of raw. When I went home and looked at my dog's dry food, which was high-end, I was appalled at the amount of fillers and lack of really substantial ingredients. That sparked the drive to create our treats with the best and only the most key ingredients—no fillers. Ever."

Treats, Glorious Treats

I'm convinced twice daily that the sparkle in my dogs' eyes can't be greater than when I'm preparing their morning and afternoon meals. And then I reach for the "cookie jar." Their anticipation sends Chief and Cinderella into begging overdrive. I tend to vary the kinds of treats I feed them so they are never sure what they will get, but they know it's going to be something good. Really good. They sink into themselves, sit or stand absolutely straight and still, their attention riveted on my hands until—hooray!—delivery is made, and they chomp it down and beg for more.

And because it feels really good to see that adoring look on our dog's face when she gets a treat, most of us give too much. Based on the ever-growing selection of treats for dogs, we are always looking for new ways to indulge our four-footed friends. Unfortunately most dog treats are like people treats—junk food—the equivalent of chips, cookies, and candy. Filled with sweeteners, preservatives, chemicals, dyes, and who-knows-what in order to make them smell like real bacon and look like mini hot dogs in buns, these treats are really not good for our pups, and they certainly aren't green!

In assessing the quality of the treats you feed your dog, go back to being the label detective you've trained yourself to be with the food for his meals. The good news is that, increasingly, dog treats are moving away from being junky and toward being healthy. There are many dog treats that feature organic ingredients and are supplemented with herbs to fight bad breath or omega fatty acids to promote healthy skin and coats. Don't be fooled by fancy packaging—perusing the ingredient list is a must, but healthy treats are out there.

TREATS FROM THE FARMER'S MARKET

If buying local is synonymous with a green lifestyle for you, then you will be delighted to know that your dog can benefit immediately from your trips to the farmer's market. Most dogs love fresh vegetables, cheese, fruit, and even nuts — all staples of the typical farmer's market. When introduced slowly, and particularly in combination with other foods dogs enjoy, diced fresh apples or pears, steamed broccoli, carrots, zucchini, mild cheese (hard or soft), and almonds or peanuts are almost always welcomed, whether as snacks or as parts of meals. With these, you also don't have to worry about over-packaging!

Baked and Served with Real Love!

Jessica Disbrow Talley shared this recipe for the biscuit that is the most popular with her customers' dogs. It contains no wheat, corn, or soy. Use organic ingredients to provide the healthiest and greenest treats possible.

Cheese Fries

1½ cups (180 g) oat flour
1½ cups (180 g) brown rice flour
1 tsp (4.6 g) baking soda
2 tsp (9.2 g) baking powder
1¼ tsp (3.5 g) garlic powder or
    granulated garlic
1 cup (113 g) shredded low-fat cheddar
    cheese
1 egg
¼ cup (60 ml) extra virgin olive oil
½ cup (120 ml) water

Preheat oven to 450°F (232°C). Combine all ingredients, reserving ½ cup (56 g) cheddar cheese to use later as a topping. Mix thoroughly until dough forms. Roll dough on lightly floured surface. Separate pieces and roll ½ x 3-inch (1.3 x 7.6 cm) sticks. Place close together on ungreased cookie sheet. Sprinkle remaining cheddar cheese on top.

Bake 20 to 25 minutes or until the cheese is lightly brown. Remove from oven. Let cool completely on a wire rack. Store in airtight container in refrigerator.

(You can check out more Bubba Rose goodies in the new *Organic Dog Biscuit Cookbook* from Cider Mill Press, 2008.)

Going Greener

So far the focus of this chapter has been on ingredients and moving from earth-unfriendly to more earth friendly. To further conserve the natural resources being spent on your dog, think about these elements:

Packaging. Consider the packaging of your favorite foods or brands of food. Is the packaging made from recycled materials? Is it able to be recycled itself? Is the food excessively packaged?

Supplements. Do you feel you need to supplement your dog's diet, or has your veterinarian recommended that you supplement to make up for a nutritional deficiency? What kinds of supplements (vitamins, oils, or special formulas) are you using, and what kind of packaging are they in? Could you find natural sources for these nutrients, or could you find local supply companies?

Water. Do you waste water while preparing your dog's meals or cleaning up after him? If you like to add some warm water to kibble, do you let the tap run until it's warm? That can waste a lot of water. Instead, fill a glass with the amount you need, and heat it in the microwave. You can better calculate the correct temperature this way, too, as you nuke it only for the time necessary to make it warm. Try to be more conscious of how much water you use filling (or refilling) the water bowl. If you find yourself dumping a lot as you replenish with cooler water, fill the bowl less full initially (and subsequently). The best water is that which is filtered to remove excess chlorine, fluoride, and other chemicals.

Dishes. If your dog eats or drinks from plastic bowls, find a way to recycle them pronto, and replace them with stainless steel or crockery. (For more on this topic, see page 122.)

Alternatives to Commercial Foods

It's clear from what's been covered in this chapter so far that feeding your dog commercially prepared food is not the greenest of choices. It doesn't mean that it's not right for your dog (or for you), and it doesn't mean that there aren't levels of green to choose from (from an organic food that's produced by a more eco-friendly company to a food made with poor ingredients by a company with a giant carbon footprint). Even with all the commercial choices available, it may be a relief to know that there are, in fact, other feeding options for dogs. These include feeding a raw diet and feeding a home-cooked diet. There are also individuals and small companies that make foods that are typically available only by mail order. They often acquire customers through referrals or advertise in specialty publications.

Raw Diets

It was Dr. Ian Billinghurst who developed the theory of raw diets for dogs and cats back in the 1990s. He coined the term that is generally associated with this kind of diet: BARF, or Biologically Appropriate Raw Food (also referred to as the Bones and Raw Food diet). The philosophy behind it is that dogs, being carnivores, should eat a diet that has served them throughout their evolution—one of raw meaty bones, offal, and fresh vegetables, supplemented with some other essential nutrients.

For those of us who were raised thinking that a bone was the last thing you should give your dog, this diet is a real eye-opener; it includes uncooked bones. Turns out that it's the *cooked* bones that are brittle and can splinter when eaten—small raw bones like those in chicken wings, for example,

are easily chewed and digested. Dr. Ian Billinghurst has written several books on the subject, as have other animal nutritionists and enthusiasts (see Resources on page 166).

Whether to feed a raw diet is a hotly debated issue with plenty of supporters and detractors. It's important to study both sides of the issue; don't just make a clean break from your dog's current diet to a raw one. If you do decide to feed your dog a raw diet, heed the advice of Dr. Bob and Susan Goldstein, and make sure the bones and meat you feed are organic. Remember that supermarket meats are largely the products of factory-farmed animals. As well as the previously discussed ills of this industry, consider the fact that meat from these animals can still contain trace amounts of hormones, antibiotics, and other toxic contaminants. Also, as the Goldsteins point out, "'Modern' methods of farming often precipitate depression and aggression, which has a definite biochemical effect on the animal's health and well-being and can translate into toxicity in the meat."

HOW GREEN IS RAW?

An organic raw diet is probably the greenest option you can choose for your dog. It steers you clear of supporting factory-farmed animals; it minimizes or negates the feeding of grains; its ingredients aren't over-processed or manufactured; and if fed properly, it has the potential to keep your dog in optimal health, reducing trips to the veterinarian and/or the need for medications.

Home-Cooked Diets

The theory behind the home-cooked diet harkens back to the days when family dogs ate what the family ate—a home-cooked meal. Those who worry about the potential for bacteria, germs, and even parasites in raw food are reassured by cooking the meats, eggs, vegetables—and often, grains—that make up this kind of diet. Again, there are pros and cons to feeding a home-cooked diet. It is an option that should be thoroughly studied before being undertaken.

HOW GREEN IS HOME COOKED?

If you go the home-cooked route for your dog, you can feel good about it as a green choice. Like the raw diet, choosing organic components is critical to its overall benefit for your dog and the planet. Because a home-cooked diet may contain many of the same ingredients you would use to cook for your family, you can ensure their source — and if you want it to be a green one, make it the farmer's market. Both the home-cooked and raw diets can incorporate homegrown vegetables, herbs, and even fruit, too — giving them extra green-ability.

Your Green Dog Food Action Plan

It's so easy to start greening the feeding of your dog. Here are some ways to jump in:

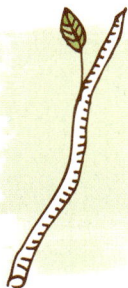

LEVEL 1

Congratulate yourself for wanting to make changes to improve your dog's health

1. Give your dog a hug and a piece of organic sliced apple.
2. Be sure you're using stainless steel or crockery bowls.
3. Be conscious of the way you use water when it comes to your dog.

LEVEL 2

1. Examine the label on the current food and treats you give your dog. Check out where and how the products are made.
2. Buy local and organic fruits and veggies. Share them with your dog.

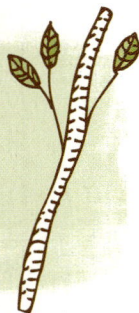

LEVEL 3

See the sidebar, 10 Simple Green Dog Feeding Fixes, and start checking off the list.

LEVEL 4

Not only are you doing most of the things in level 3, but you've started a Green Dog group in your neighborhood. You and your fellow canine con-*verts* ("vert" is French for "green") have started:

1. Buying in bulk from local farmers' markets and meat suppliers, and designating a different driver every week or so to reduce your gasoline consumption.
2. Placing group orders for any supplements or feeding supplies with a favorite mail-order company so that there is less packaging and shipping.
3. Creating and sharing favorite recipes for treats or meals.
4. Constantly recruiting other canine con-verts.

10 Simple Green Dog Feeding Fixes

You can do the following things to make a big difference in the health of your dog and to dramatically reduce his carbon paw print.

1. Reduce or eliminate reliance on commercial foods.

2. Feed whole sources of animal protein that ideally come from pasture-fed animals from a local supplier, or are at least organic.

3. Supplement with organic vegetables and fruit that come from as close to your home as possible.

4. Grow your own vegetables, if possible, and even herbs such as basil, chamomile, mint, and parsley, which are easy to grow and take up little space.

5. Share the plenty. When you leave behind the outdated (and deleterious) advice that dogs shouldn't be fed table scraps, you'll find that many of the fresh foods you prepare for yourself are good for your dog, too.

6. Be mindful of how much water you use to prepare your dog's meals or for drinking water. Don't cheat your dog out of this very essential nutrient, but don't run the tap longer than you have to.

7. Supplement with organic omega-rich fatty acids from sources such as flax seed or wild-caught fish.

8. Be sure to recycle any packaging associated with your dog's foods.

9. If you make your dog's food, store portions in glass jars with tight-fitting lids that can be reused over and over. Use glass instead of plastic whenever possible.

10. Clean your dog's dishes with nontoxic cleansers (see page 85).

CHAPTER

2

Greening
THE
Health
OF YOUR
Dog

IN THIS CHAPTER YOU'LL LEARN

What green healthcare means for
you and your dog

How to find and work with
a green veterinarian

Holistic approaches to greening
your dog's health for a lifetime

WHEN I WAS YOUNG AND LIVED IN THE COUNTRY, OUR FAMILY SHARED OUR HOME WITH A DOG NAMED GRIFFIN. He was an avid hunting dog, always in the woods tracking rabbits. Unfortunately, Griffin was allergic to fleabites. We all loved the dog, but my mother adored him. She would sit on the porch on summer evenings diligently removing any ticks he might have picked up and scouting for signs of fleas. It seemed practically impossible, however, to keep poor Griffin flea-free during the warmer months. The veterinarian suggested the options he knew and believed in: flea dips…and sprays…and flea and tick collars. Nothing worked. Eventually, Griffin's immune system was compromised, and he was given steroid shots to help with the pain and itching.

It was a pitiful sight to see our noble hound lose his hair, to feel his skin harden, and to watch his *joie de vivre* dry up. He lived to what seemed like a decent age—13—but in his final months, you could see the pain and confusion in his eyes. He couldn't stand to live in his own skin. It was heartbreaking for all of us, and excruciating for my mother, who felt she was doing what she could for him, only to see his condition worsen.

Is it possible that the medicine we used on Griffin increased his suffering and shortened his life? Personally, I think it's likely. And because of what happened to him, I'm no longer complacent about the products I use to ward off fleas and ticks on my dogs, no matter how appealing the packaging on the store shelves—or sincere the advice of a trusted professional. It's a constant battle between what might sound good and what might be best for my dogs—in the short- and long-term.

Choosing the Holistic Path

As everyone today knows, finding the best treatment options for individuals—be they people or pets—requires a lot of attention. In my opinion, a holistic approach that explores things from all angles is key (see Holistic and Green, on page 48). Like my mentor, Dr. Ian Dunbar, once told me about training dogs, "One person's system may not work for your dog; you should consider all options and go with what works for your dog *and* for you." It means more work, but better results.

As caretakers for our canine companions, we learn about care options in many different ways, and what can seem right for one dog may not feel so for another. As you read this chapter, you may have strong reactions—positive or negative—to some of the care methods presented here. Consider this your introduction to a wide range of possibilities: love 'em or leave 'em. I encourage you to explore in more detail the approaches that interest you. Discuss them with your veterinarian, trainer, groomer, and other dog-enthusiast professionals and friends. Be sure to evaluate them in terms of greening your dog's world—some may make perfect sense and be easy to achieve, and others not.

On the canine health front, no one I've met exemplifies the holistic approach more than Dr. Bob Goldstein and his wife, Susan Goldstein. They bring both a traditional and a spiritual perspective to every animal illness they confront, and they are not afraid to ask questions and challenge assumptions. I have relied on their advice for years, and they were kind enough to review this book and hash through this chapter with me.

This is not a simple subject to understand. Having green options and making green choices is complicated because treatments may depart from what you're used to doing or using. And as with any options, the greenest ones may not be those that are best for your dog *relative to a particular condition*. Caution aside, however, it's imperative for the health of your dog, your family, your community, and the planet to consider any and all green options for canine healthcare. Many options are easy to switch to, yield excellent results, and ultimately benefit everyone. Let's get started exploring them.

Choosing a Green Vet

It goes without saying that a trusted veterinarian is your greatest ally in helping your dog live a full and healthy life. He or she is someone with whom you can share concerns or ask questions and know you're being listened to, and whose ultimate concern is the health and quality of life of your four-legged companion. Hopefully this is how you'd describe the veterinarian with whom you're currently working. But how does your vet respond when you depart from conventional options and begin to share your interest in living greener with your dog?

WHAT IS A GREEN VETERINARIAN?

If you're going to look for one, it's helpful to understand what one is — or does. This is something that's still being defined in the veterinary community, so you, dear reader, have the opportunity to help shape the greening of veterinary care. The concerns you share with your veterinarian about reducing your pup's carbon paw print from a doggie healthcare perspective could affect the habits in that clinic. One day there may be a veterinary-oriented organization like the one for humans, Health Care Without Harm. Its mission: "Health Care Without Harm is an international coalition of hospitals and healthcare systems, medical professionals, community groups, health-affected constituencies, labor unions, environmental and environmental health organizations and religious groups." In the meantime, you might want to steer toward a veterinarian who employs a holistic approach. Both Dr. Bob Goldstein and Dr. Gerald Buchoff say that holistic veterinarians tend to be green-oriented, as it's more a part of their lifestyle.

Helping to Green Your Vet

Regardless of your vet's experience with green healthcare practices, he or she might be receptive to being asked about *alternative* care methods. Dr. Darren Weisenstein of 4 Paws Animal Hospital in Englishtown, New Jersey, is a conventional veterinarian who understands that each of his clients is different and might want different treatment protocols. As for going green, while he notes that not very many of his current clients ask about it, he knows it's a concern. "Veterinarians and veterinary practices," he says, "can do as little or as much along those lines as possible, whether it's reducing the amount of disposables, or recycling paper to use as kitty litter, or promoting greener products for everything from household and kennel cleaning to grooming, to rethinking vaccination protocols."

To better understand your veterinarian's position on less conventional or greener practices, explore these questions during your next appointment:

- What is your position on nutrition, especially in light of the recent pet food recall?
- What kind of vaccination protocol do you adhere to, and why? How do you feel about vaccinating senior dogs?
- What is your advice for preventing and treating fleas and ticks?
- Do you know or do you ever recommend alternative practices such as chiropractic, acupuncture, TTouch, and homeopathy?
- What kind of grooming products do you recommend?
- What kinds of diseases might my breed be susceptible to, and what measures do you suggest to prevent their onset or development?
- Are there ways that your practice is implementing green changes, such as using less toxic cleansers and supporting eco-friendly products?

Your veterinarian's responses—and the subsequent discussions you have—will ultimately lead you to make better care choices for your dog. Remember, it's *your* dog—*your* best friend—not your veterinarian's. You are your companion's only recourse for health-based choices. And one thing that holds true with any veterinarian is that your dog should be examined regularly, especially as he ages.

Choosing a Green Supplier

You may visit your veterinarian only occasionally, yet you probably go to the pet supply store several times a month. The people who own and operate the place where you shop for your supplies can be instrumental in influencing or limiting your green choices for your dog. Eco-friendly pet supply stores are emerging. At Green Dog Pet Supply in Portland, Oregon, everything from how the store was painted and furnished to what it supplies for its customers supports green living. On the East Coast, Earth Animal in Westport, Connecticut, is a standout. The store recycles 100 percent of the boxes it receives; uses nontoxic cleansers; carries toys made from organic fabrics and dyes, and beds filled with recycled bottles; offers shopping bags made from recycled paper; and actively supports other eco-friendly local businesses. Discussing green choices for your dog with the people at either of these stores is enlightening—and fun!

Preventive Care with an Environmental Conscience

To be in the best of health, dogs need regular preventive care. This includes the following routine requirements:

1. Diet and nutrition
2. All-body grooming
3. Exercise
4. Spaying or neutering
5. Regular veterinary checkups—especially in the senior years
6. Minimal stress
7. Attention. (Yes, attention is a health requirement for dogs—they are extremely social animals!)

Nutrition, Nutrition, Nutrition

This part of your dog's care is so instrumental to every other part that it simply cannot be overlooked or undervalued. What you feed your dogs, the quality of the water they drink, the things they ingest from the environment—all have an effect on their overall health. All veterinarians agree that nutrition is a keystone for good health. Fortunately for you, this book starts with a whole chapter on feeding and nutrition.

Grooming

Here's a chance to "green your cleaning," as Deirdre Imus likes to say—and has advocated in her work and writing for many years. Check her out at dienviro.com. Although her focus is primarily on children's health, what her organization has learned about the importance of using nontoxic products is relevant for our puppies, too.

🐾 Grooming Routines 🐾

REGULAR GROOMING	**GREEN GROOMING**
Brushing and/or combing the entire body, with a bath as needed	Brushing and/or combing the entire body, with a bath as needed
Cleaning around the eyes and in the ears	Cleaning around the eyes and in the ears
Brushing the teeth and checking the gums	Brushing the teeth and checking the gums
Clipping the nails	Clipping the nails

No, "Grooming Routines" isn't a misprint. The truth is that for his overall health, your dog needs to have these things done whether you choose green or not. The difference is in the products you use. Take a look at the grooming supplies you currently have on hand. What do you use that only gets used once and is then disposed of? Bath-substitute wipes, tissues, cotton swabs, cotton balls, gauze pads, paper towels, paper or plastic cups, etc.? Now think about how many of the tools you use need electricity: hair dryers, nail sanders, and so on.

Take a minute to examine the ingredients lists of the grooming products you use—everything from baby oil and doggy toothpaste to shampoo, conditioner, and so on. How many are petroleum distillates? How many have ingredients that you would never put on or near a baby? And consider this: Dr. Darren Weisenstein often sees dogs for cases of extreme itching a day or so after they have been to a groomer, leading him to believe that not only the grooming products used, but their overuse, contributes to poor skin condition.

AVOID THESE CHEMICALS

Organophosphates are found in insecticides because they poison the nervous system and lead to death for the insect. According to the Natural Resources Defense Council (NRDC) in the United States, those chemicals can also be toxic to pets and to people (especially young children). While all except tetrachlorvinphos have been phased off the market over the past few years, they are still present in some older products. The NRDC has asked the Environmental Protection Agency (EPA) in the United States to eliminate the use of organophosphates of any kind in pet products. In the meantime, avoid any products that contain any of the following:

- Carbamates such as carbaryl and propoxur
- Chlorpyrifos
- Diazinon
- Dichlorvos
- Malathion
- Naled
- Phosmet
- Tetrachlorvinphos

A Greener-Grooming Tool Kit

Acknowledging that every dog is an individual and that there is not really a one-size-fits-all solution, here is a list of grooming staples that can be used for just about every dog. Complying with it will shrink your consumption habits and improve your dog's health.

Brushes and combs. Christine Maller, an owner of Green Dog Pet Supply, says the best way to start is to think sturdy and permanent. "There aren't many brushes or combs being made for pets yet that are made from recycled products," she says, "so we recommend and stock ones that we know will last a long time. A sturdy flea comb, for example, should last for many years."

Eco-friendly shampoo. Choose ones that are biodegradable and are made without dyes, perfumes, petroleum products, alcohol, and other harsh ingredients. These are better for your dog's skin and coat, and better for the environment.

High-quality toenail clippers. Buying the best means getting the best results (a quicker, cleaner cut every time) and lessening the need for frequent replacement.

Old towels. Compared to paper towels, these are softer, more absorbent, and get better with frequent washing.

Toothbrush made from recycled plastic. Also, when brushing, be sure to use a toothpaste specially made for dogs.

Homemade coat conditioner. Put ¼ cup (60 milliliters) of organic apple cider vinegar into a quart (.95 liters) of distilled water. Shake the contents to blend them, pour some of the mix onto a clean towel, and rub your dog all over his body, being careful not to get any near his eyes. Let him shake, then brush to remove any remaining loose hairs. There's no need for disposable wipes of any kind.

Organic cleaners. Ditch the chemical-laden creams you may use to clean around your dog's eyes and ears, and switch to organic herbal-based products—or create your own blends.

KISS COMMERCIAL SOAPS GOODBYE

Most commercially available soaps — including those for the skin and hair — are formulated from a chemical soup that includes detergents, synthetic fragrances, parabens, and surfactants. These ingredients can have short- and long-term ill effects, from causing an allergic reaction to drying out the skin and coat, to the ingestion of toxins. When choosing a shampoo, look for one with herbs and natural oils as primary ingredients. Buddy Wash is excellent.

Exercise

Ask any veterinarian on any day what a key contributor to good health for dogs is, and you'll be told that exercise is at the top of the list. Sure, dogs like (and need) to sleep, but depriving them of exercise will not only lead to poor physical health, but is also a major source of behavioral problems. The phrase "A tired dog is a happy dog" was coined because it's true. And a happy dog is a healthy dog—one that needs fewer trips to the veterinarian and fewer medications, thus conserving many resources.

Run, Jump, Catch, Walk!

It doesn't matter whether your dog is large or small, either—all dogs need sufficient time to run, jump, explore, and play. If you have a dog park near you, where it's safe to let your dog off-leash to play with other dogs, take advantage of it. For well-behaved dogs, it's doggy heaven. (If you're new to a dog park, observe the dogs that frequent it before letting yours loose among them. Overly rambunctious dogs can quickly turn aggressive—a situation you want to avoid.)

If you have a dog that was bred to do a particular thing such as retrieve, herd, dig, or chase after prey, get involved in a club that does those activities with dogs. You will see a side of your dog that will bring you the greatest pride and joy as you watch his instincts take over.

One of the fastest growing dog sports is agility—your dog must navigate an obstacle course with your help and direction. It's open to all dogs of all sizes, and is great exercise for your dog and for you! Kids love doing agility with dogs, too.

And there's nothing like the long walk with your dog (or dog family!) early in the morning and later at night. Remember, though, that it's no fun for your dog if you only take him up and down the same sidewalk for a short walk every single day. Do your dog and yourself a favor, and go to a park to explore some trails. (Try not to drive too far away to do this, though, as the goal is to reduce our carbon foot and paw prints, by using as little gas as possible.) Also, remember car safety for your dog and never leave him in the car alone for extended periods, particularly if it's warm out. Hyperthermia can set in quickly for dogs and result in a most excruciating death. Discover your neighborhood by walking down roads you might not normally take. Meet up with a friend and her dog, and walk together.

And don't forget that playing with your dog inside the house or apartment is important, too. Just 10 minutes a few times a day of playing tug-of-war with your pup's favorite pull toy is good exercise for your dog, and may lower your stress, too.

EXERCISE GREEN

Knowing how much your dog (and you) can benefit from exercise, take every opportunity to walk with your dog instead of driving places. If possible, walk to pick up your Sunday paper, walk to the post office, and walk your dog when you have to get your kids at school or go to one of their outdoor games. Keep a watchful eye on your pup while you're in a store or business to make sure he's okay, and don't leave him for long. Also, when you're out and about with your dog, remember that you must pick up after him. Use a biodegradable bag to pick up the feces (there's a lot more on this subject in chapter 5).

Spaying and Neutering

In the spirit of reducing—one of the primary tenets of green living—there is nothing better for the dog population than spaying or neutering your companion. The Humane Society of the United States estimates that six to eight million dogs and cats enter shelters each year, but only three to four million are adopted. A dog or cat is euthanized approximately once every eight seconds in the United States. Spaying or neutering ensures that your dog will not produce puppies that may meet this tragic fate. It ensures that your dog—male or female—will not contract diseases associated with the reproductive organs. Males will not be inclined to roam or over-mark their territory, and females will be spared heat cycles.

Minimizing Stress

So many of us say that we would like to live the lives of our companion animals—be fed well, be permitted to sleep whenever and wherever we want, be adored by everyone, play in the mud, and so on. But are they always content? Many dogs experience stress in their daily lives. Some have just themselves for companionship for hours a day. Many are confined to crates or small rooms for hours at a time while their people are at work or out. The demands of needing to fit into a person's busy lifestyle can actually be quite stressful for dogs, and stress leads to poor health and bad behavior.

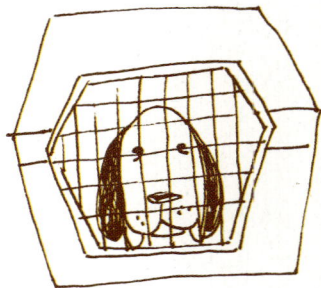

GREEN RELIEF FOR SOLO HOURS

Dr. Gerald Buchoff notes that many people leave a television or radio on for their dogs when they leave for work for extended periods of time. In his opinion, "That's an awfully wasteful activity and probably is no more entertaining for your dog than looking out the window." Playing the right kind of music can be quite beneficial, though, and studies have shown that harp music is particularly soothing. Minimize the use of other electronics so that you can keep a CD player going for even a little while during your dog's solo times. Also, a long-lasting chew toy that can be stuffed with organic peanut butter and/or dog treats is another way to keep a dog entertained and occupied when you're away from home.

Attention

Dogs are social animals, and as possible as it is to train your dog to accept staying home alone while you go to work, it's not a situation you can expect your dog to enjoy. Many of the behaviors that land dogs in shelters are a result of owner expectations that they should behave perfectly while left alone for hours on end. It's often just not possible, and a lonely dog suffers severely.

If you need to be away from home for more than four to six hours at a stretch, hire a dog walker. This could be a retired neighbor or someone who works for a pet-sitting service. This person should spend at least 20 to 30 minutes with your dog, walking and playing with it, and giving it a treat.

Green your pet sitter by choosing someone as local as possible (so long as the person or service is trustworthy and compassionate toward your friend), and be firm with your rules for picking up after your dog and using biodegradable bags.

The Vaccine Controversy

Dr. Bob Goldstein and Susan Goldstein feel that one of the greenest things a veterinarian can do is cut back on the number of vaccines they give. "There is increasing evidence," they report, "that repeated vaccinations may contribute to a weakened or suppressed immune system, which can trigger disorders as varied as arthritis, skin disease, diabetes, epilepsy, and even cancer. The potential for long-term reaction," they continue, "may be the underlying cause for many autoimmune diseases (lupus, anemia, seizures, allergic dermatitis, hypo- and hyperthyroid condition) leading to heart, liver, or kidney failure." There are even indications that some vaccinations can contribute to anxiety and other mental disorders. Not exactly the news you expect to get when you go in for your annual "booster shot" for your dog—a shot that may combine four or five vaccines in a single injection!

The Goldsteins are quick to point out that they are not against vaccinations; instead, they promote a "vaccinate wisely" protocol for their clients and customers. Puppies must be protected against the diseases to which they are susceptible, but "we never recommend a vaccine for any animal that is ill, degenerating, or immunologically compromised." They reached this conclusion decades ago, and are pleased to see many in the scientific community reach similar conclusions. The American Animal Hospital Association (AAHA), which accredits veterinary hospitals around the world and includes more than 30,000 companion animal practitioners as members, developed a task force to study the controversy surrounding vaccinations in 2003. In 2006 the AAHA published its *Canine Vaccines Guidelines*, which are "intended to educate and inform the profession and help veterinarians make vaccine recommendations for individual dogs or, in the case of a shelter, a population of dogs." The guidelines classify vaccines as core, noncore, or not recommended, and also address "serologic testing, vaccine adverse events, the vaccine licensing process, and

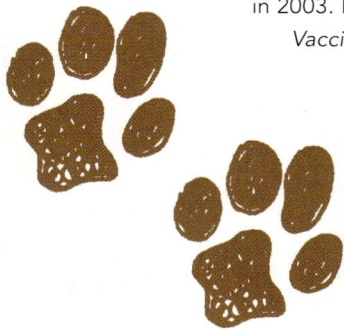

the medical and legal implications of vaccine medicine." They can be reviewed at aahanet.org/resources/guidelines_canine.aspx.

The American Veterinary Medical Association (AVMA) Council on Biologic and Therapeutic Agents published a report in late 2002 that supported an individual approach to a dog's vaccination needs. It concluded in part that "variations in lifestyles and related disease risks, and among individual vaccine products, make a one-size-fits-all protocol inappropriate."

The controversy and debate surrounding these reports, along with the findings of veterinarians around the world, have caused most vets to at least consider that an annual blanket vaccine may not be what's best for a particular dog. Dr. Darren Weisenstein says he rarely recommends a vaccine for an older dog anymore, though he feels that customizing a vaccine schedule is "a tough row to hoe," as people want their pets protected. Instead of booster shots, though, ask your vet to perform *blood-test titers* to assess the levels of immunity they still have in their systems. While Dr. Weisenstein says the high cost of blood tests is often a deterrent for a client, it's a way of assessing whether to vaccinate. He believes the call on vaccines should truly be made on a case-by-case basis.

Vaccine Detox

If you and your vet determine that a vaccination is necessary, you can minimize side effects (both short- and long-term) by detoxifying your dog afterward. There

is a homeopathic remedy for precisely this purpose: *Thuja occidentalis* helps to remove the side effects of the vaccine and prevent vaccinosis, while not interfering at all with the immunity the vaccine is intended to promote. It's usually given for five to seven days after vaccination. (See page 55 for more information about homeopathy.)

THE ENVIRONMENTAL IMPACT OF OVER-VACCINATING

Dogs that have been vaccinated (and over-vaccinated), as well as those that are regularly medicated, carry the remnants of the vaccines and their medications in their bodies and bloodstreams. When these dogs urinate and defecate, trace amounts of potentially live viruses pass through their excrement and into the environment. Whether a dog's potty spot is the backyard or a national park, multiply a trace contaminant by the millions of dogs in the United States today, and it's not difficult to conclude that these substances are all around us, every day, affecting plants and other animals in ways we may not even realize.

Holistic and Green

For those who want to reduce their dog's carbon paw print, welcome to holistic and alternative treatments. How can such a blanket statement be made? Are alternative ways, also referred to as *complementary* therapies, that seek to cure a particular ailment any more energy efficient than more traditional practices? In order to understand why they are, it's important to understand what these holistic treatments can accomplish.

The holistic approach considers illness—and wellness—from all angles: physical, emotional, and environmental. According to the AHVMA, "Holistic medicine, by its very nature, is humane to the core. The wholeness of its scope will set up a lifestyle for the animal that is most appropriate. The techniques used in holistic medicine are gentle, minimally invasive, and incorporate patient well-being and stress reduction. Holistic thinking is centered on love, empathy, and respect."

The AHVMA position continues: "This mixture of healing arts and skills is as natural as life itself. At the core of this issue lies the very essence of the word '(w)holistic.'

It means taking in the whole picture of the patient—the environment, the disease pattern, the relationship of pet with owner—and developing a treatment protocol using a wide range of therapies for healing the patient."

Here's an overview of alternative treatments.

Acupuncture

The practice of acupuncture dates back many thousands of years. Essentially, it's a treatment in which needles are applied directly to meridians in the body that correspond to areas that need relief. Dr. Bob Goldstein and Susan Goldstein explain that the insertion of a needle through the skin into a specific acupuncture point sets up a local inflammatory response. "The immune system then responds with the release of endorphins," they continue, "which further reduces inflammation." Acupuncture can be an effective treatment for a number of conditions in dogs, including pain relief, arthritis, epilepsy, urinary incontinence, and more.

In the veterinary world, interest in—and the use of—acupuncture is growing exponentially. Dr. Ava Frick, who coordinated the complementary and alternative medicine sessions at the 2007 annual conference of the AVMA, said that a decade ago you'd be lucky to get 20 veterinarians to attend a session on this topic. Today these sessions fill up fast and draw around 80 vets per session, with acupuncture and chiropractic being a couple of the most popular subject areas. Joseph A. Kincaid, DVM, has expanded the use of acupuncture in his clinic because "It's something that can be incorporated into treatment protocols to enhance results."

The International Veterinary Acupuncture Society can help you locate a veterinary acupuncturist near you—as well as help you learn more about this treatment protocol. Visit them at ivas.org. The American Academy of Veterinary Acupuncture at aava.org provides the same service.

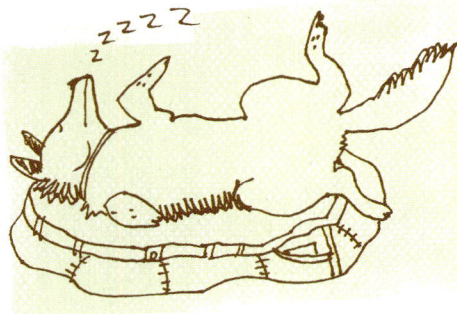

Animal Communicators

Even a holistic veterinarian may regard this complementary resource with some skepticism, and it's likely that you do, too. It can seem outrageous to telephone someone who may live a great distance away from you and has never met you or your dog, and listen as this person relates thoughts or feelings while communicating with your dog. Outrageous, perhaps, but for many, miraculous.

Our dogs can confound us with their behavior, and they can frustrate our best efforts to care for them if they have lingering or chronic illnesses that don't respond to treatment. They can break our hearts and leave us guilt-ridden when they die. So many times we feel we could help if only we could know what was truly going on by communicating with them.

Animal communicators can bring us this connection if they are truly gifted. But you'll need to be shop around carefully; as with any other kind of healer, there are effective and ineffective communicators. In their book, *The Goldsteins' Wellness & Longevity Program: Natural Care for Dogs and Cats*, the authors offer these guidelines for finding a trustworthy communicator if it's a route you want to explore:

- Does the communicator have references? Are any of the references veterinarians?
- Speak with at least three clients who have used the communicator.

- How many years of experience does the communicator have?
- What is the educational background of the communicator?
- Has the communicator published any materials, lectured, or held workshops? If so, what, where, and with whom?
- How is your own intuition resonating with the communicator?
- What is the communicator's personal mission? Is this person coming from a positive place?

Begin your search for an animal communicator by asking for a reference. If no one you know has used one, do an online search. You can start with something as simple as "animal communicator" and your state. Communicators typically put a lot of information on their websites, so you can browse their experience and credentials.

Aromatherapy

With a dog's amazing sense of smell, it's no wonder poochie can be so affected by surrounding scents. In chapter 3, you'll learn how the cleansers you use at home affect your dog through his nose, often in damaging ways. Here, however, we'll explore how aromas can have healing effects on your dog.

Aromatherapy is based on the effects of essential oils on the body. Essential oils are the essences of flowers and plants extracted through a steam process. They are actually not oily at all, and are clear-colored or slightly dark, depending on the essence. They are potent and powerful on their own, and a little goes a long way. To use them, the essences need to be combined with a carrier oil or placed on a diffuser. Aromatherapy works on a cellular level, as it's something that is brought into the body through the skin or mucous membranes of the nose.

Depending on the malady and the remedy, essential oils can work as natural antihistamines, anti-inflammatories, and even antiparasitics. They must be used appropriately, and they must be grown organically and harvested properly so the essences are themselves untainted. They should never be administered orally.

Chiropractic

Chiropractic is one of the fastest-growing alternative treatments for companion animals. The practice is based on the premise that pain is the result of an impaired nervous system, as influenced by the position of the spine. When mechanical abnormalities of the spine and musculoskeletal system can be relieved, then energy can be redirected and pain relieved.

The American Veterinary Chiropractic Association (AVCA) reports that routine chiropractic can assist dogs with conditions as varied as trouble getting up and down, seizures or neurological problems, recovery from illness or injury, chronic health problems that do not resolve as expected, and even behavior or mood changes. Finding a certified veterinary chiropractor is becoming easier as interest grows. You can search the AVCA website for referrals by going to animalchiropractic.org, or you can ask your veterinarian for a referral. Though Dr. Darren Weisenstein, a conventional veterinarian, doesn't get too many questions about how green his clinic is (yet), he is asked about chiropractors more and more, and has a referral for his clients should they (or he) feel it would benefit a particular dog's condition.

VETERINARY ORTHOPEDIC MANIPULATION

More and more veterinarians are learning the technology of Veterinary Orthopedic Manipulation (VOM) to help their patients with conditions as varied as basic lameness to incontinence and even endocrine dysfunction. VOM is not chiropractic; instead, it's "a healing technology that locates areas of the animal's nervous system that have fallen out of communication, and re-establishes neuronal communication and thus induces healing." (From the official website of VOM Technology — vomtech.com.) It was developed by Dr. William L. Inman in the late 1990s and has been taught to more than 6,700 veterinarians.

Flower Essences

"Stated simply, flower essences provide patterns of harmony that assist the body in its return to a natural state of vibrant health," says Sharon Callahan, originator of Anaflora Flower Essence therapy for animals and author of the book *Healing Animals Naturally with Flower Essences and Intuitive Listening*.

Like the essential oils used in aromatherapy and other healing treatments, flower essences are also plant extractions. Unlike essential oils, which work on a cellular level when they are applied to the skin or inhaled, flower essences are ingested orally (through the mouth) and are a vibrational medicine, working to heal by re-establishing harmonious frequencies. As Sharon Callahan further explains: "As the essence enters the physical body, it gives off a pure, harmonious frequency. The aspect that is 'out of harmony' is drawn to this healthy frequency and begins to vibrate in harmony with it."

The person who is credited with developing the healing flower essences as we know them today is Dr. Edward Bach, an English physician working at the turn of the century. He felt that one way to restore true mind-body health was to restore that critical balance, rather than use something to mask or annihilate the "disease." He turned to nature as the source for balancing elements, and he identified 38 healing flowers and plants that now constitute the Bach Flower Remedies. The most popular of his formulations is Rescue Remedy, a combination of five essences whose purpose is to "rescue" the user (human or animal) from an extremely stressful or traumatic incident—anything from a long car ride to an aggressive incident with another dog.

There are many books available on choosing and using flower essences effectively—for humans and pets. You can start your research at the websites for Anaflora (anaflora.com) and Bach Flower Remedies (bachflower.com).

BREATHE DEEPLY

Sharon Callahan has been creating flower essences for several decades. "Flower essence therapy is one of the most ancient and earth-friendly therapies available," she explains. "Just to sit with flowers in nature is one of the most healing activities we can engage in; the spirit is immediately uplifted. For animals, this is even more acute. In making flower essences, the healing property of the plant is captured through sunlight infusion and stored for future use. It takes very few blossoms to make essence, and no plants are killed in the making of the essence." With the flower essences created at her company, Anaflora, "each mother tincture (the original made in the field) will last for decades, and endangered plants and plants growing in environmentally fragile landscapes are never used."

Homeopathy

The German physician Samuel Hahnemann, the founder of homeopathy brought this practice to the Western world. Based on the principle that "like cures like," homeopathic treatment aims to reinvigorate the power of the body to heal itself. For example, a homeopathic preparation could be given at the advent of cold and flu season. By ingesting minute doses of the very substance that would bring on cold or flu symptoms, the body is stimulated to build up natural defenses to them, thereby healing itself. Amazingly, the principle is based on administration of mere trace amounts of the substances, and stronger dilutions are considered more potent.

There are now more than 1,000 homeopathic remedies available for people and animals to assist with everything from anxiety and hot spots to insect bites and upset stomachs. Learn more at holisticvetpetcare.com.

Massage and TTouch

One of the many marvelous things about dogs is that they literally beg to be petted. Our instinct is to reach out and stroke them to show our affection. In a world that is becoming increasingly touch-phobic—at least in public—physicality can be extremely therapeutic. And most dogs welcome the attention.

The intention of massage is to knead, rub, or pat the body in order to stimulate circulation. Increased circulation means better blood flow, which leads to the release of stress, improved breathing, and a general feeling of well-being. Massage therapy has been known to reduce anxiety levels of students taking exams, assist cancer patients with the effects of their treatments, lessen depression in those who are grief stricken, and improve athletic performance.

The best-known extension of the use of massage on companion animals is a system known as the "Tellington TTouch Method." It's named after its founder, Linda Tellington-Jones, and it's now taught as a course to people around the world who work with and care for animals of all kinds, from horses to birds. "The Tellington Method utilizes a variety of techniques of touch, movement and body language to affect behavior, performance, and health," according to Linda Tellington-Jones. The touches are patterns of circles, strokes, and lifts, which, when applied to certain areas, help animals become more self-confident and less stressed. TTouch can assist with problems such as fear of thunderstorms, hyperactivity, excessive barking, and any erratic behavior. Besides assisting in behavior change for the animals, it's another way to deepen the bond of trust and communication between the TToucher and the animal, which contributes to healing all around. In 2007, Linda Tellington-Jones was inducted into the Massage Therapy Hall of Fame. To learn more about TTouch and to find practitioners, visit the website at ttouch.com.

OTHER ALTERNATIVES

Some additional alternative treatment protocols include the following:

- Glandular therapy
- Hair analysis
- Herbal medicine
- Homotoxicology
- Music therapy

- Nutritional blood test (NBT)
- Ozone therapy
- Reiki
- Traditional Chinese medicine (TCM)

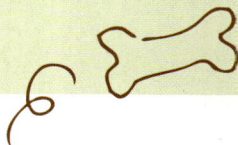

The Green Battle Plan for External Parasites

This chapter has come nearly full circle. It was a beloved dog's struggle against fleas and flea allergy dermatitis that opened my young eyes to medicine gone wrong, and that causes me to wince whenever I see products on the market that are still so potentially harmful. It's all I can do to restrain myself from removing flea and tick collars when I see them on dogs. Thankfully, there are many alternative solutions that are also much more earth-friendly.

Getting Fleas to Flee

Admit it: whenever you see your dog itching, you suspect a flea problem. I know I do. It's because the thought of eliminating not just the fleas on my dogs but on any surfaces they have trod on fills me with dread. The truth is, by the time a dog is itching because of fleas on his body, chances are they are well established in the home or on the property. To prevent this nasty situation, you need to do three things for the best results:

1. Improve your dog's diet to boost the immune system.
2. Regularly go over your dog with a flea comb, especially in warm weather.
3. Keep your house and yard clean.

A Holistic Approach

While attacking the problem from the outside by eliminating existing fleas may seem logical and timely (and in many cases it is), if you think about it, you'll also realize that there is even more sense in the holistic approach: consider healing from the inside out at the same time you work from the outside in.

Studies have shown that parasites prefer an unhealthy host—one that is sick or older. The first line of defense against fleas and other parasites, then,

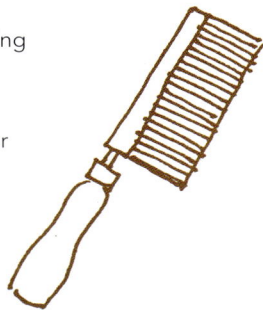

is to bolster the immune system, which makes your dog less appealing to fleas to begin with. See chapter 1 for specifics about improving Spot's diet.

The debate rages on about the effectiveness of brewer's yeast, garlic, or a combination of the two. Dr. Bob Goldstein and Susan Goldstein are proponents of this combo, but warn that brewer's yeast and garlic in themselves are not magic bullets. Be selective about the type of brewer's yeast you choose—find one that is fresh and strong smelling. Fresh garlic is beneficial for overall health as well as being a deterrent for parasites, but it can also thin the blood and should not be overused. Consider supplementing with some *super foods*, too, such as wheat grass, spirulina, or super blue-green algae. B vitamins and minerals are necessary, as well.

Now work from the outside: regularly groom your dog to keep his skin and coat in the best condition and to check for itchy or sensitive spots. Go over him with a flea comb during peak conditions for fleas. Next, focus on keeping your house clean. Vacuum and sweep daily, if necessary, during the warm weather. Fleas lay their eggs on a host, and the eggs, as well as flea larvae and pupae, drop off the host. The tiny pupae hide in carpets, under your dog's bed, in the dust along the walls, and under the radiator, etc. They hatch when they're disturbed: when someone walks on them, when your dog lays down on them, when the vibration from footsteps jostles them—and they immediately seek out a host (your dog or you or someone else in the family) to nibble on and start the life cycle over again. That's how a flea problem perpetuates itself. Nasty business.

ANOTHER ORGANIC COMPOUND FOR FLEAS

To assist in the battle for control of fleas in the house and yard, there's diatomaceous earth. Otherwise known as "DE", it's a powder made from the microskeletons of diatoms, which live in the ocean. The super-fine powder works by dehydrating the exoskeleton of the flea, which kills it. DE won't harm dogs or cats, and is effective on the animal, in carpeting, and in the yard. You can find it in some garden centers, health supply stores, or online.

Giving Ticks the One-Two Punch

Ticks are another tiny external parasite with the potential to cause major problems—witness the epidemic of Lyme disease over the past few decades. It's spread by the deer tick and named after Lyme, Connecticut, where it was first diagnosed. There is a vaccine for Lyme disease—like other vaccines, it should be given only after considering all options, as over-vaccinating can cause much more harm than the protection you may be seeking. Whether you vaccinate or not, ticks are a pest to be reckoned with, as they can be difficult to find until they've bitten and feasted on your dog, at which time they expand and are easier to see and feel. Once bitten, there is always a chance that your dog has been infected with a tick-borne disease.

Treat ticks in the same manner as fleas, by boosting your dog's immune system and keeping them off poochie and out of your house and yard. After every outing with your dog during tick season, spend a few minutes examining him for ticks. Do this outdoors or in a mud room away from the main house. Getting as many as you can before your dog settles in the house is key! Have a glass jar filled with isopropyl alcohol handy. When you remove the ticks, put them in the jar and replace the lid tightly when you're finished. Needless to say, keep this jar well out of the reach of children (anyone, really). When the ticks are dead, dump the jar in a far corner of your property and flush the spot with water, too.

If a tick has bitten and is attached to your dog, you need to remove it carefully to get the full tick. Numb the tick and assist the skin in fighting the germs by dabbing it with apple cider vinegar. Use tweezers to get as close to the mouth as possible. Pull firmly but gently. Immediately dispose of the tick in the alcohol-filled jar and cap it. Treat the bite with apple cider vinegar and antibiotic ointment. Watch your dog for symptoms of infection, such as irritation around the wound, lethargy, soreness, or any unusual behavior.

ESSENTIAL OILS TO DETER TICKS

Dr. Gerald Buchoff cites essential oils as potent preventives for keeping ticks at bay. One that he recommends is rose geranium. A few drops on a cloth or nylon collar can repel ticks with no toxic effect on your dog. The owners of Earth Animal agree and also advise people to use citronella in the same way. Remember, though, that essential oils are potent — a little goes a long way — and they are not appropriate for the feline members of your family!

Getting Mosquitoes to Bug Off

Mosquitoes are a problem for outdoor-loving people and their dogs. Their bites sting and can cause itching and welts. Now there is also the chance that a mosquito will transmit the West Nile Virus through a bite, though wild birds, horses, and humans are the ones most commonly infected, and it's rare (though possible) for dogs to fall prey to this disease. What these nasty bugs can transmit to dogs, however, is the parasite *dirofilaria immitis*, or heartworm. Ingested from another animal, the larvae travel through the mosquito's bite into the bloodstream of a dog, where they take up residence in the heart and lungs and begin to grow. Heartworms can reach lengths of 1 foot (30.5 centimeters) and will clump together, effectively blocking blood flow and stopping the heart.

Because a heartworm infestation is difficult to treat effectively, the veterinary community created a preventive medication that is prescribed for dogs living in areas where it's a consistent threat. Today it's common for dogs across the country to be on a monthly preventive medication year-round. But is ivermectin—the common ingredient in heartworm medication—safe for long-term application?

According to Dr. Bob Goldstein and Susan Goldstein, when it comes to matters of the heart—the most vital organ in the body—it's better to be safe than sorry. Especially if you live in a high-risk area, the conventional therapy makes sense. If you don't, you can consider combining a conventional with a natural approach. Consider giving the medication every six weeks instead of every four, and as always, supplement the diet to support the immune system. Give garlic regularly (no more than two cloves a day for a large dog), and look into adding a parasite-specific homeopathic formula, such as Earth Animal's Internal Powder (earthanimal.com).

The American Mosquito Control Association has a website, mosquito.org, where you can learn more about West Nile Virus in particular. It created a catchy play on words to help people protect themselves from mosquitoes. It's a 3-D approach: Drain, Dress, and Defend. *Drain* any freestanding water around your home; *dress* in light-colored protective clothes (darks attract mosquitoes; long sleeves and pants cover more skin); and *defend* by using repellents (select natural rather than chemical products).

Dr. Goldstein's Green Battle Plan for Internal Parasites

Theories abound on what the most effective natural approaches are for repelling pests. So much depends on the particular environment and (of course) the kind of dog you have. Since I defer to Dr. Bob Goldstein on matters such as these, here are his recommendations.

The bugs that can harm your dog from inside his body include roundworms, tapeworms, hookworms, and whipworms. Coccidia and giardia are microorganisms that can make your dog sick, too. Most are transmitted through the feces or unclean environments shared by other infected animals. Symptoms of infection run the gamut from a potbellied appearance to vomiting, diarrhea, loss of appetite, or poor skin and coat condition. Detection is made through microscopic examination at a veterinary lab.

Diet, Diet, Diet

The greenest approach to ward off these internal parasites is to keep your dog in the best of health. Again, it's garlic to the rescue! It helps reduce the buildup of mucous in the body and is a natural repellent. Garlic won't kill an existing infestation, but it will assist in preventing worms from embedding themselves in your dog's vital organs. Remember that dairy products are mucous producers, and keep these out of your dog's meals, treats, and snacks.

The medications used to deworm dogs are potent and leave in their wake harmful by-products in the environment. By boosting your dog's immune system and avoiding potentially infested areas, you may not need to resort to these drugs.

Your Green Dog Health Action Plan

The goal of this chapter is to get you started thinking about ways to go greener with your dog's healthcare. It touches on the aspects of care that are most common—preventive measures, internal and external parasites, and alternative approaches that can improve your best friend's overall health. Bigger issues like cancer, allergies, or diseases of particular systems are so very important to understand from every perspective possible, and are beyond the scope of this book. With the information provided here and in the Resources section on page 166, you can go on to learn more about addressing these serious issues in ways you may not have considered before—ways that could not only benefit your dog, but the planet, as well.

In the meantime, you can now choose to adopt some of the methods discussed below:

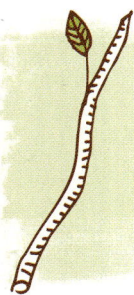

LEVEL 1

Congratulate yourself, and take a close look at your dog. If you begin using the advice in this chapter, you're in for a wonderful surprise when you see how your dog begins to thrive. Here are two action steps you can start today. Both will improve your dog's health and your positive attitude! Improved dog health is a very green strategy.

1. Commit to giving your dog more exercise and playtime.
2. Recognize your dog's attention-getting behaviors for what they are and tune in to him. Play his favorite game with him for five to ten minutes, sit on the floor and whisper sweet nothings in his ear, push the other thoughts from your mind, and pet him calmly and quietly. You will both feel less stressed and more energized through these simple acts of connection—or reconnection.

LEVEL 2

Some simple things you can do include:

1. Re-evaluate the products you use to keep your dog clean, and explore more natural alternatives.
2. Reread chapter 1 and recommit to doing more when it comes to providing a better diet for your dog.
3. Log on to ahvma.org and see if there are any holistic veterinarians in your area. Consider going for a consultation if you've never been to one before.
4. Commit to working with a veterinarian who supports a greener perspective. You need a professional ally.

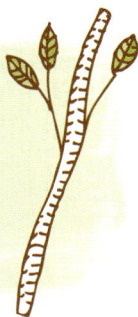

LEVEL 3

You can do the following things to make a big difference in the health of your dog and the health of the planet.

1. Don't over-vaccinate. Consider your dog's life stage and find out the dates of his last vaccinations. Get titers done to assess the level of immunity and confirm the need for additional vaccinations.
2. Ditch any grooming products you currently use that contain potentially harmful or earth-unfriendly ingredients (see page 39)—or that come in wasteful forms such as disposable wipes—and choose natural-based, earth-friendly products instead.
3. Banish toxic flea and tick remedies from your home. Just say "No!" Make it a habit to check your dog for ticks and fleas after every outing or get-together with other dogs. Keep your flea comb where you'll pick it up and use it without having to search for it.
4. Figure out an alternative to the monthly heartworm medication your vet may be prescribing for your dog "just

because." Be honest with your vet; let him or her know that you want to stay on top of keeping your dog heartworm-free but also that you don't want to over-medicate with conventional heartworm drugs.

5. If you haven't done so already, spay or neuter your dog.

6. Take the time to find a reputable animal communicator (see page 50) and go ahead: treat your dog and yourself to a session. You won't regret it.

LEVEL 4

Be part of the green dog revolution. Where healthcare is concerned, this could include the following:

1. Talk to your veterinarian or veterinary group about greening the office or clinic. Using less toxic cleaning agents is one simple but significant step toward making any clinic a healthier one for all the dogs (and other animals) they treat. By taking that action themselves, they are influencing clients to do the same.

2. Develop an herbal-based mosquito repellent so effective that you want to share it with your dog-friendly family, neighbors, and coworkers.
3. Form a group of like-minded dog people to support your own forays into alternative therapies and to keep each other apprised of new developments, eco-friendly products or initiatives, and so on.
4. Become active in supporting studies that question how often vaccinations should be given. One that's been initiated by Dr. Jean Dodds, Dr. Ronald Schultz, and Kris Christine is the Rabies Challenge Fund, which seeks to address "the duration of immunity actually conveyed by rabies vaccine…finance a study of the adjuvants used in veterinary vaccines, and establish a federal adverse reaction reporting system for rabies and other vaccines." Check it out at rabieschallengefund.org.

WORDS TO LIVE BY

This is a lot of information, especially if you're just beginning to explore less conventional methods. Dr. Bob Goldstein and Susan Goldstein sum up how to approach your dog's healthcare this way: "While high-tech veterinary medicine can be a lifesaver, the routine reliance on multiple drugs and chemicals will gradually wear down your animal's liver, kidneys, and other organs of detoxification. It's far better to support the immune system with healthy foods, targeted supplements, fresh pure water, and plenty of exercise and affection daily." (From **The Goldsteins' Wellness & Longevity Program: Natural Care for Dogs and Cats.**)

CHAPTER

3

Greening Your Dog House—

THAT'S *YOUR* HOUSE!

IN THIS CHAPTER YOU'LL LEARN

How to do an overall home assessment

Options for green cleaning

How to make greener choices for
your dog—and yourself

FOR THOSE OF US WHO LIVE WITH DOGS, OUR HOUSES JUST AREN'T HOMES WITHOUT THEM.

What better way to begin or end the day than with the loving greeting you get from your best friend—your dog? Who's happiest to see you come through the door—even if you've only been gone long enough to take out the trash? You know who—your dog.

There are almost45 million canine-caring households in the United States and nearly 90 million dogs living in them, according to 2007 statistics from the American Pet Product Manufacturers Association (APPMA). Where do you think most of those faithful friends are waiting while we go about our busy lives? In our homes, of course.

The nice thing about greening your dog's house is that—as the title of this chapter reveals—you're greening your own home at the same time— a two-for-one deal that benefits both of you (and whoever else shares your home). That's great motivation. So where to get started?

There are many elements to consider when you decide to green your home. The choices can be as simple as eliminating one or more of the toxic cleansers you currently use, or choosing green building materials when you redecorate. Let's explore what a green makeover could mean for your home—and the environment you and your dog live in.

Home Assessment

Take a walk through your house—your dog will be happy to join you. As you go through each room, think about the following:

- Cleaning products
- Air quality
- Floors and floor coverings (carpets, area rugs)
- Lighting
- Types of fabrics used throughout the house for curtains, dog beds, human beds (including mattresses and pads), upholstery, and so on

Now go to where you store your cleaning supplies and look at the kinds that you use. In her book, *Clean & Green: The Complete Guide to Nontoxic and Environmentally Safe Housekeeping* (Ceres Press, 1994), Annie Berthold-Bond assesses the primary ingredients in common cleansers. In just one frightening example—that of commercial toilet-bowl cleaners—she writes,

"May contain: Complex phosphates, o- or p-Dichlorobenzene, chlorinated phenols, kerosene, salicylates, germicides, fungicides, 1, 3-Diochloro-5, sodium acid oxalate, sodium acid sulfate."

"Toxicity: Sodium acid oxalate, cholorinated phenols, and o- or p-Dichlorobenzene are highly toxic. Sodium acid sulfate is highly corrosive. Chlorinated phenols are not only corrosive but metabolic stimulants. Fungicides can cause liver and kidney damage…"

Do you use a commercial toilet-bowl cleaner? Does your dog drink from the toilet? Consider that many of these same ingredients are in other commercial household cleaners, too, which means traces of them are on your clothes, your bed linens, your furniture, your upholstery, your carpeting—and the dog bed.

Sensitive Paws

When you think about it, dogs are much more vulnerable to the effects of the surfaces of the home than we are. Though the pads on their paws are tough, dogs essentially walk around barefoot all the time. This means that after you've mopped the kitchen floor or walked in from outside wearing shoes that track street grime into your house, if your dog pads along beside you, the residue from the floor or from your shoes can get onto his feet. Chemicals can leach through the skin or, worse, when your dog lays down and licks his paws, the chemicals can get onto the more sensitive and receptive cells of his tongue and gums, gaining easier access to the bloodstream than by absorption through the paws.

BREATHING IT IN

Dogs have a highly acute sense of smell. This amazing ability has been harnessed in many ways to help humankind, from search-and-rescue dogs and seizure-detecting dogs to dogs that sniff out illegal substances in airports. Depending on the breed (or mix), dogs can have up to several hundred million odor-detecting cells in the mucus of their nasal passages (humans typically have ten million or fewer). They also have an active vomeronasal organ at the roof of the mouth that further heightens their ability to detect and differentiate scent. One of the exercises in competitive obedience is to present a dog with a large group of objects, any one of which has been touched by his handler. Without having seen his handler touch that object, the dog must identify it — within a matter of seconds — by scent alone.

In your own home you've probably seen this ability in action when you leave a piece of candy or other snack at the bottom of a bag or briefcase. You forgot it was there, but your dog won't leave the bag alone. When you go to explore why, there's the candy (unless your dog gets it first!). As you use cleansers around your house, on the places where your dog sleeps or eats, on the items your dog wears, or even on his fur or skin, imagine the impact that scented products — meant to please us scent-immune humans — have on our canine companions.

Fragrance Free
please!

Examining Air Quality

With your dog's scent-sitivity in mind, think about the overall quality of the air in your home. If there's a smell that's bothering you, think about how it might be affecting your dog. If you're the kind of person who enjoys air fresheners, scented candles, the smell of detergents, and so on, you don't necessarily need to eliminate these things, but you may want to start experimenting with cleaner, greener scents.

For example, do you love the smell of fresh citrus fruits such as lemon, grapefruit, or orange? Slice one in half, squeeze it onto a natural sponge, and place the sponge on a countertop that's out of the way. If this seems too all-natural for you, or you're looking for a more permanent or long-lasting air deodorizer, consider placing mesh bags of zeolite in the rooms you and your dog frequent most often. Zeolite is actually an abundant form of volcanic rock that attracts odor molecules with its negative charge.

If you know air quality is a problem in your home and you need even more help than odor eliminators or fresheners can provide, consider an air purifier. There are now solar-powered models for those who are reluctant to plug in yet another appliance.

A LITTLE VENTILATION GOES A LONG WAY

For a dog who is confined to a crate for several hours at a time while his family is out of the house, it's important that there be sufficient air circulation in and around his den. Wire crates with openings all around are probably best. To provide a safe and secure feeling in the crate, be sure there is plenty of padding on the bottom, and drape a cloth that is breathable—yet blocks some of the light—over the top of the crate and partway down the sides. A bamboo sheet makes a great cover.

Examining the Floors

One significant but often overlooked contributor to poor air quality is carpeting, and this is where I'll begin our examination of flooring. Wall-to-wall carpeting, while it can look great and feel wonderful, is in essence a vehicle for trapping all kinds of dirt and debris. Carpet fibers can trap mold, bacteria, and other allergens; anything tracked in on your shoes can find its way deep into the fibers; and odors from cigarette or cigar smoke, frying, and chemical cleansers also live in carpets.

Carpet Concerns

As grownups we may not spend too much time in close contact with the carpeting in our home, preferring to get around on two feet, with our heads 5 to 7 feet (1.5

to 2.1 meters) up from the floor. But dogs—especially small dogs—are intimately associated with the carpets in our homes. They walk on them in "bare feet," they fall asleep and breathe deeply on them, they roll on them to scratch themselves, and they even eliminate on them (despite our disapproval). Dr. Bob Goldstein and his wife, Susan, have treated animals for liver and kidney issues and have been able to trace the illnesses back to newly installed carpets that the animals slept on! Did you ever notice that new-carpet smell? It's the result of all the chemicals that are used to produce and treat the materials. If you're getting a good whiff of it, then you know that your dog is taking a huge hit.

Another fact about carpeting—especially wall-to-wall—is that people don't keep it around for very long. It gets replaced for any number of reasons, including irreparable damage from repeated accidents by our beloved canine companions. Carpets and their conventional pads, made from foam or synthetic rubber (which is itself created with petroleum products), end up in landfills by the billions of pounds per year.

SLIP-SLIDING SENIORS

For those fortunate enough to share a home with a senior dog — considered to be age eight or over — it's sad to watch our friend struggle to get onto or stay on her feet. Just as the degeneration of the body affects old people who move more slowly and with greater caution, it affects old dogs, as well. If you have slippery floors — wood, tile, linoleum — consider placing an area rug (with a lining that will keep it from slipping) in high traffic areas or in places your dog likes to hang out. This can prevent a senior dog from taking what can be a painful and sometimes dangerous spill that could require additional medical care. A simple area rug made of natural fibers can be a comfort and a safety for an elderly dog.

What's a Rug-Lover to Do?

Fortunately, there are now many green rug and carpet options that even the choosiest of decorators can live with. There are rugs made from natural fibers, including coir (spun from coconut husks), cotton, jute, linen, sea grass, sisal, wool, and a wool and hemp blend. The padding that goes under carpets is now being made from recycled and renewable fibers, too. As interest grows, so do the number of styles, colors, shapes, and sizes. Home Depot even has an Eco Options brand dedicated to products that have lowered impacts on the planet (homedepot.com/ecooptions). Lowe's has its line of "Healthy Home" products, too.

The Floors Themselves

If a walk down the aisles of a D-I-Y big-box store has you worried about finding eco-friendly building supplies, worry not! Construction is an industry that is quickly greening itself, and there are many options for people who are remodeling or considering building something new. Here are three websites that are obvious places to start: greenbuildingsupply.com, greenbuilding.com, and buildinggreen. com, which even has a television show (buildinggreentv.com).

Deciding to change the kind of floors you have is a big decision. In a nutshell, what you need to know is that bamboo, cork, Marmoleum (a linoleum-like product made with all-natural ingredients), and reclaimed wood are your greenest bets. Linoleum is actually biodegradable, but still has associated VOCs. Vinyl used for flooring is polyvinyl chloride (PVC), the life cycle of which (from product through a product's usage time) has been identified as one of the most toxic of consumer goods.

Not all of these green options are a good fit for active dogs: for instance, bamboo scratches fairly easily.

Cleaning the Floors

No matter how green your floors or floor coverings, dirt happens—especially when you have a dog or dogs (and maybe additional pets) sharing your home. If you're going to opt for a greener floor and floor coverings, you need to think about how to care for them. This means using the proper cleaning products and tools. (See Resources, page 166.) For now, let's take a look at vacuum cleaners, dry mops, and other common tools.

Suck It Up!

A dog owner's best friend—or worst enemy—can be the vacuum cleaner. It's the front line of attack for dirt, hair, dander, and other junk your dog may track in and leave around. If you have dogs, it's virtually impossible to get by without a vacuum (personally, I would not even want to try). Yet a vacuum can also be an energy hog, and an inefficient vacuum can blow as much dust back into the environment as it attempts to suck out.

There are many, many, many, many, many vacuums available these days, and choosing one can often feel like a horrible compromise between what you know would do a great job and what you think you should pay. The wording on this is deliberate, because if you've shopped for a vacuum recently after not needing one for awhile, or if you're going to be purchasing a vacuum any time soon, sticker shock is sure to be a part of your experience. A *good* vacuum is expensive. There's just no way around this.

As a dog owner—and especially as one with a green side—you must have a good vacuum, one that has the following benefits and features:

- Does a very good job of cleaning, which can translate into needing to run the vacuum less frequently
- Contains a HEPA filter to better trap what you're sucking up (see below)
- Has a bagless option so you can eliminate the cycle of buying and disposing of vacuum-cleaner bags

If you're going to make a major investment in a vacuum, talk to someone with experience. There are fewer and fewer of them, but if you're lucky enough to live near a store that just sells vacuum cleaners, call and talk to the owner. Chances are this person has been in the business for a while. The next best thing is to check out a site like bestvacuum.com for ideas.

WHAT'S A HEPA FILTER?

HEPA stands for High Efficiency Particulate Air. Applied to a filter, it's a designation that indicates that the filter can trap 99.97 percent of airborne particles that are 0.03 micrometers in diameter (the hardest kind to trap). So exact is this measurement that only filters that truly measure up can be called HEPAs (imitations are referred to as HEPA-type or HEPA-like). HEPAs trap particles larger than 0.03 micrometers with even more efficiency.

Lighting Is Illuminating

I'm sure you know that one of the easiest and most effective ways to save energy and live greener is to change the kind of light bulbs you use in your home, from incandescents to energy-efficient compact fluorescents (CFLs). We are reviewing this information here in our green dog book because—well, it's something all of us who care about Planet Earth can do.

The fact is that about one-quarter of the energy consumption in the United States is spent on lighting, so it's no wonder that making a simple change from incandescents and halogens to CFLs is a no-brainer. While incandescents last about 750 to 1,000 hours, CFLs, which use about 75 percent less energy, last about 10,000 hours. This is a significant saving for a homeowner's budget, and it reduces the pollution of the planet. China, which makes about 70 percent of the world's light bulbs, agreed in October 2007 to begin phasing out the use of incandescents for replacement with energy-efficient CFLs and other options, with the potential to offset its carbon emissions by 500 million tons (510 million metric tons) a year. The initiative is being backed by the Global Environment Facility (GEF). Australia is also phasing out incandescents and GEF is working with other countries to do the same.

Leaving the Light on for Fido

Many people who leave their dogs at home while they go to work leave at least one light on. Whether or not the house would be blanketed in darkness otherwise, having at least one light on makes it look less abandoned from the outside and, it can be argued, helps people and animals in the house feel less isolated when it's dark outside. How further reassuring to know that a CFL bulb left on will use significantly less energy. If the brightness of the bulb is a concern, remember that CFLs use about a quarter of the wattage of an incandescent. A comparable CFL wattage for a 60-watt bulb would be about 15 watts.

The Fabric Connection

Now that you've walked around and looked closely at what's in each of your rooms, I'll bet you never realized how many types of fabrics surround you. The ones you want to pay particular attention to are those that cover furniture or bedding, as these are the ones you—and your dog—come into contact with the most.

Fabrics designed to take the beating of frequent use or exposure are often treated with chemicals to resist staining, minimize odors, retard fire, and increase durability. They often cover cushions or pads made with polyurethane foam, itself a highly flammable petroleum product that is treated with a host of chemicals.

Dog Beds

Providing comfortable, convenient, attractive—even luxurious—beds for our dogs has become a modern-day necessity. Scratchy baskets, oversized cardboard boxes, or hand-hewn wooden boxes padded with old sheets and blankets simply won't do for today's pampered pups. It's easy to find faux-fleece crate pads, overstuffed nesting beds, and extra-large, sofa-like loungers piled high with everything from fine fluff to orthopedic foam. Doctors Foster and Smith, one of the largest pet supply mail-order catalogs, sells more than 70 different types of beds in a variety of colors, many with interchangeable covers. Companies including L.L. Bean, Orvis, and Cabela's include dog beds in their product lines. Dog beds are everywhere!

Dogs do love dog beds (and people beds, and people furniture), and they have their favorites. Mine have been known to argue over one that's in my kitchen; and it's first-come, first-claimed at night for the dog beds in my bedroom. If you're like me, many of the photos you have of your dog are of him fast asleep on a dog bed—so angelic and peaceful.

Enjoy the pictures and save them to look at years from now because what you're going to discover about what most dog beds are made of is decidedly unpeaceful. Things are starting to change, for sure, but for now most dog beds (and mattresses for babies and adults) are made with some form of polyurethane foam or polyester fiber (a common product is Polyfil). The Polyurethane Foam Association (PFA) acknowledges that "brominated and chlorinated fire retardants comprise about 90 to 95 percent of the foam industry's typical fire-retardant usage." A bill introduced to the California legislature in early 2007 is seeking to eliminate the use of both these fire retardants in the production of foam. The chemical substances in petroleum are used to make polyester fibers, plastics, and films.

Plastic bottles are also made from petroleum-based materials. Often, recycled plastic bottles are made into polyester fibers. While this certainly helps, it's startling to discover that of the four million plastic water bottles Americans use every hour—yes, hour—only one-quarter of them are recycled.

EVEN COTTON CAN BE ROTTEN

If you think you're making a more natural or green choice by selecting cotton fabric over polyester, there's one word that can make it true: organic. If the cotton you select isn't organically grown, it's the product of an industry that is one of the most pesticide- and insecticide-intensive in the world.

What do you do when your dog has an accident on his bed? You can remove the cover and wash it; if the mattress is made of polyester-fiber, you can attempt to wash it, too, though you need to be careful in the drying process to prevent it from ending up clumped and lumpy; and if the mattress isn't washable, you can try to get as much of the odor out as possible with water and an enzyme stain and odor remover. If the problem continues or intensifies, chances are you will want to dispose of the bed and start over. More trash generated. More nonrenewable products consumed. Fresh chemicals in and on the bed, and right up your dog's sensitive nose.

THE COVER COUNTS, TOO

If you're going to pay attention to what's inside your dog's bed, you should take note of what is covering the contents, too. Many synthetic fibers create additional static on your dog's skin and coat, especially in dry homes in the winter. Materials that claim to be stronger, inhibit odor, or resist staining are probably made with additional chemical treatments to support those claims. What do you want near your dog's skin?

Green Dreams

You may want to find a piece of organic cotton that you can fashion into a cape for your dog, because his search for a green dog bed is going to make him a superhero. It's challenging, but it's worth it. Rather than going the easy route of searching online, take your crusade to the streets. Call the store or stores where you typically shop for your dog's supplies and tell them you want green choices. Dog beds are being made with bamboo, hemp, organic cotton, and recycled materials. If you demonstrate the demand, the supply will come. Talk about sweet dreams!

STARTLING STATISTICS

Treehugger.com reports that the U.S. power grid is 98 percent nonrenewable energy (51.7 percent coal, 19.8 percent nuclear, 15.9 percent natural gas, 7.2 percent large hydroelectric, and 2.8 percent oil).

Green and Clean

The reasons to reevaluate your cleaning products are so obvious when you consider them. Let's see…

- Ammonia is caustic and poisonous if swallowed. It's a common ingredient in kitchen and bathroom cleansers.
- Another common ingredient in scouring powders is chlorine. Chlorine and ammonia combined produce a toxic chlorine gas.
- Disinfectants commonly contain chlorine bleach (also called sodium hydroxide or sodium hypochlorite), which is fatal if swallowed, and caustic to the skin and eyes.
- Conventional soaps are made from petroleum products.
- Synthetic fragrances, used in virtually all cleaning and personal-care products, are compounds derived from petroleum. They're capable of causing allergic reactions and other medical problems.
- How comfortable are you with a product the label of which announces, "Caution: Keep out of reach of children and pets"?
- How comfortable are you with products that have been tested on animals?

Now think again about your dog. Powerful sense of smell. Closer to the floor. Walks around inside and out with no covering over his paws. Likes to investigate things with his mouth. This may explain why veterinarians are seeing increased incidences of the same kinds of problems that pediatricians are dealing with: allergies; rashes; diseases of the eyes, ears, nose, and throat; lung, liver and kidney disease; and cancer.

VOC PERVASIVENESS

From epa.gov/iaq/voc.html: "EPA's Total Exposure Assessment Methodology (TEAM) studies found levels of about a dozen common organic pollutants to be two to five times higher inside homes than outside, regardless of whether the homes were located in rural or highly industrial areas. Additional TEAM studies indicate that while people are using products containing organic chemicals, they can expose themselves and others to very high pollutant levels, and elevated concentrations can persist in the air long after the activity is completed."

Clean Sweep

Have you rid your kitchen and bathrooms of the cleansers the ingredient panels of which are filled with user cautions and lists of unpronounceable chemicals? I have! It pains me to think that the liver cancer that claimed the life of my German shorthaired pointer Exley, at the young age of 11, could have been due in part to the amount of time he spent indoors on synthetic materials that had even more chemicals applied to them to clean them. Or that my sweet white shepherd Chelsea, whose increasingly frequent accidents were attacked with an army of conventional cleansers, may have suffered more as a result. It's a sad and guilt-inducing way to think, but it's also a motivator to make changes for my current companions, Chief and Cinderella (not to mention my husband and sons), starting now! Did you know that common furniture polishes are potentially so toxic that they have killed household birds? I didn't until Dr. Bob Goldstein and Susan Goldstein informed me about this.

The cleaning products I use the most are an all-purpose cleanser, a degreaser, furniture polish, window cleaner, linoleum floor cleaner, dishwashing liquid, dishwasher detergent, and a toilet-bowl cleaner. It turns out that making sound substitutions for these products is actually pretty easy. What follows are two ways to do it:

1. Choose commercially available products that are biodegradable, nontoxic, and free of synthetic fragrances and dyes. Companies making such products include Ecover, Seventh Generation, Dr. Bronner's, Deirdre Imus Greening the Cleaning, Restore Products, and Begley's Best.

2. Make your own cleaning formulas (see the recipes on page 86) with household ingredients that are biodegradable, nontoxic, and certainly free of synthetic dyes and fragrances, though you can add natural fragrances (see page 51) that can actually benefit rather than potentially harm every member of your household.

Recipes for Homemade Green Cleaners

The basic ingredients you need to tackle most routine cleaning jobs are probably already in your cupboards: white vinegar; baking soda; salt; a vegetable oil-based liquid soap (such as a coconut oil-based or castile soap); and tools that include cotton rags, cheesecloth, spray bottles, newspapers, and a bucket. You can also experiment with the astringent properties and invigorating scents of citrus fruits (lemons in particular), as well as herbs and essential oils.

An excellent solution for cleaning a linoleum floor is to put about ½ cup (118 milliliters) of white vinegar in a gallon (3.8 liters) or so of warm water. A similar vinegar-water combination can be put into a spray bottle and used on windows. Simply rub the liquid off with newspapers (as odd as that may seem).

For stains on rugs, club soda is a good product to start with. An application of dry cornstarch can sometimes lift a spot, or try a salt-and-vinegar combo with one part salt and two parts vinegar. After applying and rubbing in any one of these solutions, allow it to sit for a while before vacuuming up the residue. Your dog will think he's in the streets of Ireland getting fish-and-chips—how great is that?!

Especially for Doggy No-Nos

You may be thinking that all the club soda in the world won't remove the combination of a urine or feces stain and the awful smell left behind on your favorite Oriental carpet. And you're right. The double-whammy with these kinds of stains is that dogs—again, with their remarkable sense of smell—consider a urine spot a mark to return to over and over again unless the odor is completely eliminated. This can be very frustrating!

The best approach to removing the stains and odors of urine or feces is to take immediate action. First, clean up as much of the mess as possible. Blot up as much urine as possible by placing layers of newspaper over it (or, if necessary paper towels and newspapers) and standing on them until they've absorbed as much as they can.

Next, apply a cup or two (237 to 473 milliliters) of warm water into which you've added about a tablespoon (15 milliliters) of a cleansing liquid such as castile soap.

Put this on an old, clean towel and then blot the stain with it. The next step is to apply a mixture of white vinegar and warm water (using a one-to-two ratio), blotting after the application. Cover the area with a towel and allow it to dry. This can take six hours or more. Finally, vacuum.

If you can still smell something, use an enzyme stain and odor remover, but be careful when using it on wool rugs, as the enzymes can break down the wool. You might also want to try a bacteria digester.

For odor removal, try placing a bag of zeolite in a corner of the room, where it can be kept out of view of people, and out of the range of a dog's paws, nose, or tail. All the while, sing a happy song to the dog star, Sirius, and ask for understanding in getting through these kinds of situations with your beloved companion. It's not easy!

Your Green Dog House Action Plan

You've chewed through all the information in this chapter and hopefully gotten some good ideas. Keep the momentum going—act now!

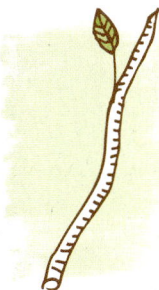

LEVEL 1

1. Congratulate yourself and give your dog a hug. There are some very exciting changes in store that will have you both breathing easier.
2. Improve your dog's air quality right away by getting light on scent: toss the commercial air fresheners and candles that contain heavy synthetic fragrances.

LEVEL 2

1. Replace your incandescents with compact fluorescent lights. This simple act will help your entire household. Your dog will be proud of you!
2. Replace the toxic cleansers in your home with as many eco-friendly products as possible.
3. Start researching vacuums that will do a better job than the one you use now.

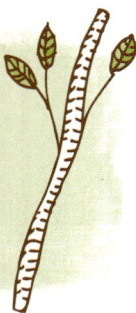

LEVEL 3

You have done everything in Level 2. Now you're ready to:

1. Identify the rooms in which your dog spends the most time, and make every effort to green those first (they're probably the same rooms you spend the most time in).
2. Choose natural fiber area rugs as floor coverings whenever possible. Also seek out greener carpet mats. Dogs need traction on the floor, or they can slip and fall, which can cause joint and muscle problems.
3. Purchase home improvement products that are as low in VOC off-gases as possible. This includes cabinets, countertops, furniture, paints, wall and floor coverings, and so on.
4. You've bought a fantastic new vacuum cleaner! Everyone is breathing easier.

LET SLEEPING DOGS LIE—IN A GREEN BED!

Using organic cotton, bamboo, or hemp material, sew a simple sack with a zipper. Fill it with clothes that might otherwise end up in the landfill because they're too stained or torn to go to a consignment store. This can include solo socks, old T-shirts, even faded jeans. Wash the clothes first, and then stuff the sack with them. Voila! A comfy...and green...dog bed for the pooch!

HOME SAFETY IS GREEN, TOO

When you're considering changing larger elements of your home, such as flooring and bedding, as well as the cleaning products you use, don't forget that little things contribute to the overall green-ness and therefore health and safety of your dog. If your dog has access to dangerous things in your home, it won't matter if his dog bed is eco-friendly. In examining your housekeeping, remember to protect your dog from the following:

- Trash
- Medications — prescription and over-the-counter
- Foods that are bad for dogs, including chocolate, macadamia nuts, and grapes
- Electric cords
- Antifreeze and other products for cars/motors

LEVEL 4

Not only are you doing all the things in the previous levels, but you've started a green dog house group in your neighborhood. You and your fellow canine con-verts have started to…

1. Take The Mantra "reduce, reuse, recycle" to the dog bed, dog toys, dog house—you name it, you can probably remake it from your stash of stuff in the garage. For example, why not make a dog bed out of old clothes?

2. Host a green cleaning party for a few like-minded friends so that you can start mixing and experimenting and sharing ideas. Next thing you know, your whole neighborhood will be cleaning green.

3. Work with your pet store personnel to bring in greener products. Review the household stain and odor removers on the shelves of the stores near you. Take a look at the kinds of dog beds they offer. What about educational materials—they could use a book like this one!

CHAPTER

4

Greening
Your Yard

IN THIS CHAPTER YOU'LL LEARN

How to do an overall yard assessment

How to start greening your yard
for your dog

How to maintain a dog-friendly and
eco-friendly yard

A YARD—LARGE OR SMALL—IS A VERY IMPORTANT PLACE FOR DOGS. It's where they most frequently eliminate, making it distinctively *their* place. It's where games are played, cookouts are held, gardening happens, time is taken to relax, children do all kinds of things … in a nutshell, it can be a paradise for your dog (and your family). What you might not be aware of is how far from paradise the typical yard can be when you look a little more closely at the kinds of things that are used in it and on it. This chapter will give you advice on how to create a *real* paradise in your own backyard, one that provides all the sanctuary and enjoyment you, your dog, and the planet deserve.

Yard Alert

Greening the outside of your home can be tackled in a similar manner as greening the inside: it starts with a walk and an assessment. Take your dog. He loves it when you poke around the yard with him.

1. Start at the back door. What do you walk out onto: A patio? A deck? A walkway? Dirt? Grass? A sidewalk? Take note of the material that you walk on when you enter and exit your abode.

2. Now look around your yard. Do you pride yourself on your lawn and try to keep it lush and green, weed-free, and manicured?

3. What kinds of plants do you have in your yard? Do you grow any fruits or vegetables? Do you water them frequently or fertilize them?

4. How do you dispose of the waste your dog leaves in the yard?

5. Is the yard fenced for your dog?

6. If you put your dog in an enclosed run that's just for him, how do you keep it clean?

7. Can your dog get in and out of the house on her own and be inside a safe enclosure?

8. Is there shade or a doghouse outside?

9. How do you manage outdoor parasites such as fleas, ticks, and mosquitoes?

From the Ground Up

Begin creating your backyard paradise by examining it from the ground up, starting with the soil, then considering the size and type of lawn you'd like, as well as ornamental or functional plants. From there, you should consider what to do about the walkways, patio, or deck, and what you will use in your yard.

What's Coming Up?

Knowing the chemical composition of your soil will help you a lot when you start thinking about what's growing in it (or not). If what's there isn't looking too good, either your soil is really depleted or the crop on it is incompatible with the soil type. Especially when you have a dog or dogs, you need to have the right stuff planted on healthy soil, or your yard will take some real paw-nishment.

Down and Dirty

It's funny that our instinct to correct the appearance of something most often leads us to put something else over it, or to approach the problem from the outside in. For example, a skin blemish gets treated with an ointment; a wall gets painted; problems get solved by talking about them; and gardens are beautified through the use of chemicals. While these are practical and sometimes necessary solutions, there's another element to a fix that can go unconsidered, and that is what's inside or beneath the surface. Proper nutrition that contributes to better health may reduce the incidence of skin blemishes, finishing a wall with a textured surface may mean it doesn't need to be painted, self-examination may reduce problem behavior, and naturally healthy soils may produce gardens that are self-sustaining.

It's on this last point that we begin our journey toward greening the yard, as the soil that makes up your piece of paradise is where it all begins.

SAFETY IS ALWAYS GREEN

It won't matter how eco-friendly your yard is for your dog if he's not kept safely in it. An enclosure is only as trustworthy as the people who come in and out of it (consider a self-closing contraption on the door or gate that closes off your yard, especially if you have children), and the only way your dog can be reunited with you if he escapes is if he is properly identified. Therefore:

1. Make sure your fencing is secure and that the gate people pass through into your yard closes properly.

2. Make sure your dog always has his collar on when he's out, and that there is an identification tag on it that gives his name, and your home and cell phone numbers.

Healthy soil will naturally withstand the onslaught of weather extremes, from cold to hot and wet to dry. It will support a cover crop of an indigenous plant or plants. Healthy soil inhibits the occurrence of disease and pest populations just like a healthy body will. You may be lucky enough to have healthy soil already. You may have unhealthy soil that needs to be restored to health. Or you may live where there isn't any soil to speak of—where scraping off a bit of topsoil reveals sand or rock beneath. Regardless, for a *green* yard (not necessarily including green-colored grass), you have to make the most of what's there.

To better understand what you're working with, explore in more detail a few spots in your yard. Dig a foot (30.5 centimeters) or so down and look at the composition of your soil. Take a soil sample, and take or send it to the nearest cooperative extension office. It will test your soil to determine its current chemical composition. In the United States, you can find the office nearest to you by going to csrees.usda.gov/Extension/index.html.

UN-GREEN EFFECTS

The price United States residents pay to have their lawns look picture perfect is high. Consider these statistics from the National Wildlife Federation (NWF) and the Environmental Protection Agency (EPA):

- More than 67 million tons (60.8 million metric tons) of fertilizers and pesticides are applied to residential lawns and gardens annually.
- Yard waste makes up about 20 percent of municipal solid waste.
- Depending on the city, 30 to 60 percent of urban fresh water is used to water lawns.
- Ten percent of U.S. air pollution is generated by lawn and garden equipment (including five percent from lawn mowers alone)

PUTTING THE PUZZLE TOGETHER

Architects start with drawings of what the final structure will look like (down to the details), and so should landscapers —and face it, if you have a yard you're a landscaper, because you have to make the yard look like something! With a dog, you need to think about landscaping even more, because some natural patterns that dogs follow may dictate what you should do. Being as green as possible with your yard means choosing options that are as low maintenance and as eco-friendly as possible. Those are a lot of elements to juggle!

Are you pleased with what's growing in your yard at the moment? Are you pleased with how your yard looks? If you're serious about greening your yard, consider the following questions:

- How often do you water your yard?

- Do you use chemical fertilizers or pest control?

- If you have grass, how often do you mow it?

- Do you use fuel-powered lawn mowers, weed whackers, leaf blowers, and snow blowers?

- How do you manage your dog's waste? (Notice how this question comes up a lot? In fact, I've devoted an entire chapter to this topic, starting on page 110.)

The truth is, the more you minimize or eliminate the need for fuel-powered mowers, trimmers, leaf blowers, and snow blowers, the more you can reduce fuel consumption, cut back on carbon emissions, cut down on using chemicals, use less water, and better manage your dog's waste (there it is again!). All these things contribute to a *greener* yard. If you're worried that even cutting back on the treatments you give your yard to keep it looking good may result in dehydration, deterioration, or devouring (on the part of bugs or disease), you're actually a prime candidate for the suggestions in this chapter.

GAS-POWERED MOWERS

According to the EPA, a traditional gas-powered lawn mower produces as much air pollution as 43 new cars, each being driven 12,000 miles (19,312 kilometers). It has now been calculated that lawn mowers contribute about 5 percent of the air pollution in the United States—more in urban areas—and that some 800 million gallons (3.1 billion liters) of gas fuel mowers every year.

What's a Lawn-Lover to Do?

If there's simply no substitute for a lush patch of green lawn in your life, you don't necessarily need to deny yourself. Instead, put it in perspective. What if you reduced the overall size of your lawn oasis, making it the centerpiece of an otherwise *greener* kind of garden and yard? Instead of grass stretching from one side to the other (no matter the overall size you're working with), consider blocking it off and surrounding it with greener options. Make it a size that you can tend with the new generation of reel mowers (see Reel Mowers on page 98); then use hardscaping options such as pebble, brick, concrete, or flagstone walkways or patios. Think about how your dogs move around your yard. Chances are they like to explore the periphery to investigate what's going on beyond their property. Often the dog's frequent movements along a fence line will create a dirt path—that's a great place to put a walkway!

Getting back to your lawn oasis, the greenest option is to make sure you plant a type of ground cover that thrives with the least amount of tending. Talk to local nurseries and garden centers about the types of grass that do best with the least amount of care. The same goes for plants you may want to put along your walkways. Always opt for those that are most resilient for your type of climate.

REEL MOWERS

Inexpensive, low maintenance, pollution-free, safe, and quiet. Are these words you'd normally associate with a lawn mower? Today they can be, if you invest in a reel mower (a push mower). Unlike the kinds used before there were electric- and gas-powered mowers, today's push mowers are lightweight, easy to operate, and effective. So what are the cons? You can't push them over sticks or expect them to chop up and compost leaves. And you can't let your grass get too tall before you mow it (but you won't be letting this happen anyway, since dog-loving parasites inhabit tall grass).

If you have a large yard, consider letting part of it go wild or support a crop. Sowing a percentage of your yard or property with indigenous grasses, wild flowers, wheatgrass or ryegrass—or a combination of these—can have a number of beneficial effects. Not only can these plantings take less effort to care for and provide natural beauty, they can also attract beneficial insects and other wildlife that your dog will love to watch.

ORGANIC OPTIONS FOR FERTILIZING LAWNS

The primary culprits in the death of lawns are the weather (too hot or too cold), weeds, and grubs. The first can be managed by choosing the right kind of grass for your area. If it's right, it should be resilient to temperature extremes. Droughts can wreak havoc on lawns, but watering to keep them looking picture-perfect is particularly eco-unfriendly. In fact, watering incorrectly can cause even further harm. A regulated irrigation system is a good option, as is watering in the early morning. As for controlling weeds and grubs, more and more organic options are available. Corn gluten meal is a weed inhibitor and fertilizer that is completely safe to use. It should be applied in early spring to be effective. Milky spore powder is a bacteria that targets the grub stage of Japanese beetles, eliminating them before they mature into adults that feast on all kinds of plants. An online search for these products and other organic gardening remedies will yield a lot of results.

Be Water Wise

Watering vast expanses of lawn may produce a green look, but it's not a *green* action. While most of us take fresh water for granted—the daily per capita usage in residential areas of the United States is nearly twice that of Europe (92 gallons or 350 liters versus 53 gallons or 200 liters)—many people in the world need to seek out fresh water every single day. When there are so many simple ways to save water, it becomes almost unconscionable not to. Here are eight ways you can make a difference:

1. Water only in the early morning or the evening, when the water is least likely to be evaporated by the sun or heated air.

2. Avoid watering when it's windy, as the water will be blown away from its target.

3. Collect rainwater in rain barrels. Put them under the drains of your gutters to make collection even easier and quantities greater. This water can be used to feed plants, dilute dog urine and waste, wash the car, or rinse off garden equipment.

4. Make sure any hoses or watering cans you use are intact. Repair any places where there are leaks. This goes for faucets, too.

5. If you must use a sprinkler or irrigation system, put it on a timer so the water is on for only a limited amount of time.

6. Don't use the hose to clean your walkways or driveway; instead, use a stiff broom.

7. Mulch your flower beds, trees, and other plantings to help hold water in the ground, as this will reduce the need for watering.

8. Choose plants that don't need that much water. Your local extension of the government's agriculture department or a reputable nursery can help you select them.

Dealing with Dog Waste

When my husband and I lived in New York with a dog, we did what had to be done: several times a day we took Exley out on a leash so that he could relieve himself. This meant getting dressed immediately upon waking up in the morning (you don't want to walk around the neighborhood in your pajamas), rousing ourselves from that near-comatose sleep late at night to take another trip up and down the block, and being prepared for any kind of weather. When we moved to the suburbs, the part of our property that delighted us most was—can you believe it?—the fenced yard! We still went for walks around the neighborhood, but those early-morning, late-night, or weather-inhibiting walky times were no longer needed. Instead, we just opened the door and let Exley do his thing in the yard. Joy!

Of course, we weren't completely off the hook. It didn't take us long to realize that if we didn't stay on top of picking up in the yard, it was soon a maze of what we called land mines...those piles that didn't seem to go away...even in a pouring rain...those piles that kept us from enjoying the wonderful yard we had so looked forward to...those piles...

Dog poop has such an impact on the environment that there's a whole chapter devoted to it in this book (see page 110). To help you with your yard, consider the following:

DOO DILIGENCE Try to get out there and pick up after your dog at least every other day, or you will soon be overwhelmed.

DOO SOMETHING There are several ways you can remove the

piles. You can use plastic bags (biodegradable, of course), scooping up with one, placing what you pick up into another, and then putting both bags in the trash. You can use a pooper scooper to pick up the piles, although this necessitates a disposal bag or a waste digester system to finish the job (for more information see page 115).

DOO OVER A waste digester system can be purchased from a pet supply store or catalog. It's a lidded container that gets put into a hole in the ground. You place the piles inside, and then add an enzyme digester and water. The waste is broken down and disperses into the ground.

DOO IT RIGHT For fewer surprises in the yard, train your dog to use a designated potty spot. Create an area that will be comfortable and convenient for your dog to use but that's some distance from where you spend most of your time in the yard. You will need to spend time training him to use the spot, and you'll need to maintain it so it doesn't gross out you or him, but if you can manage this, it makes life simpler and cleaner.

WHAT TO DO ABOUT URINE

This can be a greater woe than feces because it can leave areas of dead grass in your yard. The best solution is the designated potty spot, which will confine the problem (see above). The only other thing you can do is try to get to the spot soon after the incident and dilute the urine with some of the water from your rain barrel. There are many products on the market that can be applied to the yard or given to your dog to help control the effects of the urine on the grass. Buyer beware, however. Are they safe? Are they effective? Are they worth it? In my opinion, they are not — especially if you have an eye on being green. Why purchase or use unnecessary items? Why risk compromising your dog's health? Why apply anything more to your lawn?

What to Walk On

A patio or deck is an important feature of a yard. It provides a solid surface upon which to place furniture, as well as aesthetic appeal. For your dog, a patio or deck with a shady spot can provide the perfect retreat, and is cleaner and healthier for him than the hole he's bound to dig in the bushes if he doesn't have a cool spot to lay down in during those dog days of summer. If you're planning on building a patio or deck, explore green options through sites such as buildinggreen.com, greenbuilding.com, or the website of the U.S. Green Building Council, usgbc.org. The EPA has an incredible site that includes an extensive listing of GreenScape options: epa.gov/greenscapes.

What to Relax On

The best way to go green on your deck or patio is to give new life to old furniture. Check your local classifieds for listings or visit websites such as craigslist or ebay to see if you can find anything. Yard sales, antique shops, consignment stores, and tips from real estate agents who know of people who are looking to get rid of large items such as furniture are all potential sources for your next set. Give the old furniture a face-lift with eco-friendly paints and finishes, which you can also find online or even, increasingly, at hardware and do-it-yourself centers.

Another option is to find furniture made with recycled plastic lumber. Plastic lumber is more durable than pressure-treated lumber and is relatively maintenance free, as it won't crack, warp, or mildew. In a 2003 report done by the Tellus Institute and available on the EPA's website (epa.gov/epawaste/partnerships/greenscapes/pubs/lumber.pdf), the comparable cost of an 800-square-foot (74-square-meter) deck built from plastic lumber versus pressure-treated lumber resulted in significant savings over a five-year period. The initial cost of the plastic lumber is greater, but the wood is costlier to maintain.

More and more outdoor spaces are including floor coverings, too. For dog owners, selecting these with a green conscience is even more important, as dogs will be laying their whole bodies down on these surfaces for extended periods of time, whereas we just put our feet on them. Outdoor rugs need to be weather resistant like the furniture around them, and this is where natural fabrics and those made from recycled materials can really shine. Jute, hemp, recycled plastics—all make excellent choices for outdoor rugs. Avoid wool, of course, and be sure that if you use a pad, it's a green choice, as well.

Last But Certainly Not Least: Pests!

Chapter 2 (see page 32) included information on the kinds of pesticides commonly used to rid dogs of fleas, ticks, heartworms (carried by mosquitoes), and other parasites. Since the great outdoors is the initial source of these bugs, no discussion of a yard that's also green for your dog is complete without touching on the topic here, too.

It's an unavoidable fact: Pests can be present in your yard, and they can make their way onto your dog or otherwise infest your dog while he is outside. No flea-control program is sound if it does not include information on how to treat your yard or any outside areas your dog frequents. As anyone knows who has had to deal with the unhealthy annoyances of ticks and fleas—much less a potentially fatal heartworm infection—it's enough to tempt you never to let your dog outside!

The advice in this book will help you minimize your dog's pest problems. The result will be a happier and healthier dog—and a more hospitable yard and home. Your human family will be happier, too (does anyone *like* fleas?). If you follow the suggestions on page 58 about how to make your dog less palatable to pests, soon you may be able to stop using the toxic, chemical-filled pest-control products on the market. To green your yard and to make it unfriendly to fleas, ticks, and mosquitoes, read on:

- Keep your lawn mowed. High grass is a favorite hiding place for ticks.

- Identify and control any areas where freestanding water accumulates, as these are breeding grounds for mosquitoes. These could be in the driveway, in a recessed part of the yard where the kids (two- and four-legged versions) have worn down the grass around their playground, in planters around your deck, and so on. Improve the drainage around the areas, or repair them by filling them with small stones or simply emptying or moving the water after a heavy rain.

- Hang up a couple of bat houses (check out batconservation.com for information about where to hang them). If you're lucky enough to attract bats to your bat abode, you'll be rewarded with way fewer bugs: bats feast on insects, especially mosquitoes.

- Sprinkle food-grade DE (diatomaceous earth) on dry parts of the yard, for example along the edges of the house or barn. It will kill fleas, but the product is otherwise harmless (see page 58).

- When venturing farther than your yard or after spending time outdoors around dusk and nightfall, be sure to wear protective clothing, and check your dog (and yourself) for any freeloading pests before you reenter the house.

Your Green Dog Yard Action Plan

You've chewed through all the information in this chapter and hopefully gotten some good ideas. Now keep the momentum going: start making some changes right away. There are all sorts of ways to go about it; here's some help.

LEVEL 1

As each chapter reemphasizes the basic tenets of making green choices for your dog and you—*reduce, reuse, recycle*—you're probably starting to see and do things differently without even thinking about it. Where your yard is concerned, your first thought was probably to dump any chemical fertilizers or pesticides you may have been stashing somewhere, or to double-check your faucets and hoses. You're a green go-getter!

LEVEL 2

Some simple actions to fulfill this level include:

1. Having a soil test done on your yard.
2. Visiting your local agricultural branch of the government to explore more area-appropriate plants for your garden.
3. Using biodegradable bags to pick up after your dog in the yard.
4. Embracing a more tolerant position on urine stains in the lawn, and tossing anything you've been giving your dog or putting on the grass to control these.
5. Looking for used patio furniture online rather than driving around to stores to find new furniture or accessories.

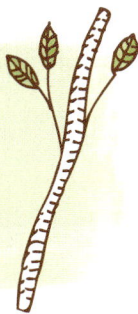

LEVEL 3

You can do several things to significantly reduce the impact you and your dog have on the yard:

1. Reduce or eliminate the size of the area in your yard devoted to a lush, green lawn.
2. Choose the type of grass that is best suited for your soil and your geographic area, as it will require the least amount of help to thrive.
3. Choose green building materials as you make all present and future landscaping decisions.
4. Replace dog paths—those beaten-down tracks your dog has created by running along the same parts of the fence day after day—with brick, stone, or poured concrete walkways. They will look better, wear better, and lead to tracking less dirt into the house.
5. Choose the most eco-friendly and green products possible when you need to fertilize or target a problem in your yard or garden.
6. Stop using at least one of your fuel-driven yard tools—the leaf blower, the weed eater, the snow blower, maybe even the lawn mower.

LEVEL 4

Not only are you doing most of the things in Level 3, but you've started a green landscaping group in your neighborhood. You and your fellow canine con-*verts* have started to:

1. Create a blog for your cooperative extension service to help others in your area choose the best plants for water conservation and decoration.
2. Talk to the managers at your local hardware stores, nurseries, and big-box do-it-yourself stores about stocking more recycled, organic, and earth-friendly lawn and landscape items, including building materials.
3. Mow your yard with a reel mower…ask your kids to mow your yard with a reel mower…ask your dog to mow your yard with a reel mower—now wouldn't that be wonderful?!

CHAPTER

5

Doo-ing
THE
Green Thing

IN THIS CHAPTER YOU'LL LEARN

Why picking up after your dog
is so important

Options for greener waste maintenance

How to green-up after your dog

WHEN I WAS LITTLE, MY FAMILY TRAVELED TO FRANCE FAIRLY OFTEN BECAUSE MY MOTHER WAS BORN IN PARIS. It was in that most glorious of cities that I learned to both revile and marvel at what dog waste can make people doo—I mean do. The French are notorious for their love of dogs, *et pour quoi pas?* They take their pooches with them to many more places than even Americans do. In restaurants, in stores, in markets, and of course on every street in Paris you see *les chiens*—and *les chiens* typically behave very well. While this can make for a very friendly city, it can also make for a very dirty city. As a little girl, I learned to keep one eye on the city and the other on the sidewalk.

One of the strangest contraptions I ever saw in the 1970s was a motorized poop picker-upper—called a *crottoir*. (*Crot* translates as "crap," and a *trottoir* is a sidewalk.) This vehicle, which looked like a miniature zamboni for smoothing the ice on rinks, would ride along the sidewalk squirting at and suctioning up the *crot du jour*. Amazing! Today in Paris there are people who wear green jumpsuits and ride on motorcycles specially equipped with tanks and suction hoses that do what the crottoirs used to do. *Mon Dieu!*

GREEN DOG, GOOD DOG

A Stinky Situation

Paris's solution to dealing with dog waste seemed silly and exaggerated to me until recently. Growing up in the country rather than the city, I was used to dogs doing their thing at the perimeter of the yard or in the woods. It wasn't something my family had to deal with. When I lived in the city with a dog, I became a plastic-bag carrier and did what was expected of me: I scooped, knotted, and tossed the goodies into a trash can. Now that I live in suburbia, I continue to clean up with plastic bags. All the dog walkers around me did—and do—the same.

LET'S PICK IT UP

Big dogs doo it
Little dogs doo it
Even dogs that live in high-rises doo it
We may not want to doo it
But let's pick it up!

(Sung to the tune of "Let's Fall in Love" by Cole Porter.)

What to Do?

For years using plastic bags has felt like the responsible thing to do. And in the face of the plastic bag overuse crisis, it felt for a time almost more responsible, as it was a reuse option for the plastic bags. But not today. I am now acutely aware of the impact of dog (and other pet) waste on our ecosystem. The plastic bags we are showered with at most retail establishments are not biodegradable—and we use 50 to 80 billion of them a year, according to the National Resources Defense Council (NRDC). Filled with dog poop, the bags accumulate and fester in landfills, becoming rock-hard for the ages.

The problem of keeping sidewalks, yards, and parks clean of doggy debris, no matter the size of the city—or yard, or park, or dog—is one that won't go away. If we love dogs and we keep dogs, we must clean up after them or risk living in putrid conditions. What the green movement is helping to make us all more aware of, though, is that things aren't necessarily "out of sight, out of mind." Even when it comes to the rather vile task of picking up, it isn't over just because the pile is off the street or the ground.

MOUNTAINS—AND RIVERS—OF MOVEMENTS

It's estimated that American dogs produce about 10 million tons (9.1 million metric tons) of feces a year. Waste that is not picked up is eventually washed away into storm drains and waterways, compounding their contamination with other runoff that has high levels of bacteria.

Technology to the Rescue

Paris, France, came up with a system to try to handle its dog waste problem, so it's apparent that other places are grappling with the issue on a collective rather than individual basis. San Francisco, California, is another city flush with dog lovers (no wonder it's such a great place!). It's also an eco-minded place that already has a food-scrap recycling program to benefit farms and vineyards, and a goal of diverting 75 percent of its waste from landfills by the year 2010. Since a study revealed that nearly 4 percent of what was in San Francisco's landfills was pet waste, it seemed a clear area to target.

Norcal Waste Systems, based in San Francisco, initiated a project to recycle dog waste into methane gas to use as a substitute for natural gas to power things such as heaters and stoves. Norcal distributes biodegradable waste collection bags in high-traffic dog areas such as Duboce Park. The waste is brought in carts to centralized digesters, which work like the dog refuse septic systems frequently used by homeowners (see page 115). Over the course of several weeks, anaerobic digesters break down the waste, creating methane gas, as well as compost that can be used on gardens.

Toronto, Canada, also has a goal of diverting 70 percent of its waste from landfills by 2010. In a study of contents found in park bins in the summer of 2006 by that city's Parks, Forestry, and Recreation Division, it was determined that about 25 percent of the refuse was dog waste. Several options were put in place to alleviate the situation in the summer of 2007, including asking dog walkers to use plastic bags provided by the park, take their dog waste home with them, or use in-ground bins that would be cleaned by septic waste managers. It was found that providing disposal bags was helpful in at least keeping parks cleaner.

What You Can Doo

Using poop-scooping plastic bags is still the most practical and efficient way to at least get the waste off the ground and to a place where it won't run off into a local water system. To make the practice a bit more earth-friendly, companies are introducing biodegradable bags. While you wouldn't want to use these on long walks or in very wet weather, for the typical short walk in the park or scoot around the block they are excellent. Some of the products even come in specially made dispensers that can be attached to your dog's leash or collar so you can't forget them on your outings. (See below for a list of these products.)

BIODEGRADABLE POOP BAGS

Hopefully these will be as easy to find in the grocery store some day as non-biodegradable bags are today. Imagine the difference it would make to our planet if everyone used them in place of non-biodegradable bags in our garbage cans, for snacks and sandwiches, as leaf disposal bags, and so on. Here's a list of products and sources, though it's certain to expand:

BIO BAGS 100 percent biodegradable and compostable; biobagusa.com

FLUSH PUPPIES 100 percent biodegradable; flushpuppies.com

POOP BAGS 100 percent biodegradable and available in a variety of sizes; poopbags.com

ECOBIO DOGGIE BAGS 100 percent biodegradable and compostable via the oxi-biodegradation process; ecosafeplastics.com

THE FLUSHABLE BAG 100 percent biodegradable; wisconsinpetproducts.com

DISPOZ-A-SCOOP 99 percent biodegradable; the bag attaches to a piece of cardboard so you don't need to put your hands around the waste; nice idea and nice bag, but the additional cardboard also needs to be disposed of, which detracts somewhat from its green-ness. It's still a good idea, though; www.healthpronutrition.com

Doggy Dooley

A great way to dispose of the piles your dog leaves in your yard is in a Doggy Dooley digester system, available at many pet product websites and retail stores. It works like a septic system: you drop the waste and some enzymes into the contraption, and it takes care of the rest. There are different sizes for different needs. Most pet product stores or mail-order catalogs carry them, or you can do an online search. You can also create your own yard disposal system by digging a hole at least four feet (1.2 meters) deep and far enough away from any wells or areas where water runs or accumulates—and away from any vegetable gardens. Place a secure lid over the hole (something that can't be easily dislodged unless you lift it, such as flagstone), and toss in the waste. You're essentially burying the feces in your backyard. If you want to do this, research the technicalities first!

Depending on the way your sewage is treated where you live, flushing your dog's feces down the toilet is the greenest solution, especially if you have a water-monitoring system such as a Bowl Buddy in your toilet—one that keeps flushes to a minimum. This way the dog waste is treated in the same way as human waste. Some biodegradable bags can be flushed along with the poop; check the instructions on the package to be sure.

WHAT NOT TO DO WITH DOG POOP

Even if you don't get around to implementing a single idea in this chapter, what you as a responsible dog owner (one of millions) must do is be mindful of your dog's messes. So remember the following:

Do not leave your dog's waste on the ground—even in your yard. Unless you live in a remote area, the dog population is simply too high, and the waste will run off into—and contaminate—the local water systems.

Do not put dog waste onto your organic materials compost pile. The average composter does not get hot enough to break down the pathogens in dog poop.

Do not use newspapers to clean up after your dog. The paper won't properly contain the waste, and it will contaminate the trash around it.

Your Green Dog
Doggy-Doo Action Plan

Okay, it's certainly not the most tasteful of topics, but cleaning up after your dog is essential. It can—and should—be done in an eco-considerate manner. Here are your options in a nutshell....er, biodegradable plastic bag.

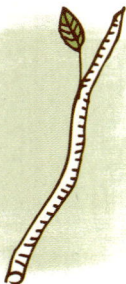

LEVEL 1

1. Always pick up after your dog!
2. Purchase and use biodegradable poop bags (see page 114).

LEVEL 2

1. Install a doggy refuse septic system in your yard (see page 115).
2. Suggest to other dog walkers that they pick up after their dogs.

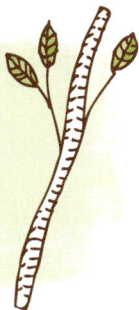

LEVEL 3

1. You offer other dog lovers disposable bags; yours is a "No waste left behind" policy that inspires others.
2. You flush your dog's waste as often as possible into a toilet that's outfitted with a Toilet Tank Bank or other water-saving device that limits the amount of water produced with every flush.

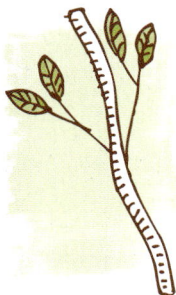

LEVEL 4

Dutiful to the nth degree with the actions listed in Levels 1, 2, and 3, you're motivated to help others do the same. Here are some things you could do:

1. Meet with the store managers of your local pet supply retailers and talk to them about carrying biodegradable bags.
2. Suggest to pet supply retailers that they designate an area for plastic bags to be returned for recycling—donating these to a park for use as scoopers could make a difference.
3. Organize a Canine Earth Day for your neighborhood. Break out into groups that cover the parks and streets, picking up dog waste and other trash. Have business cards made up for your group so that when people see what you're doing, you can give them a card with information about the importance of picking up after dogs and the statistics relative to waste in landfills.
4. Learn French and launch a website where Parisians can log on and learn how to start making changes in their city. Though I haven't been to Paris recently, those who have tell me the streets are still "sale" (dirty)—even with the people on patrol. Maybe it's time for a chien vert revolution.

CHAPTER

6

Greening
THE
Goods
OF YOUR
Dog

IN THIS CHAPTER YOU'LL LEARN

How to provide your dog
with green supplies

When to apply the *reduce, reuse, recycle*
mantra to the things in your dog's life

How to cultivate a less = more attitude

DON'T TELL YOUR LOCAL PET SUPPLY STORE, BUT THE GOAL OF THIS CHAPTER IS TO HELP YOU FIND AND PURCHASE ONLY THE NECESSITIES FOR YOUR DOG. This isn't an easy thing to do in our consumer-oriented world, where every day brings new sales circulars to our mailboxes (what a colossal waste of paper!) and the barrage of products we're tempted to purchase keeps expanding. When it comes to shopping for our dogs, the temptation to buy and try new things can be even greater, as it's a known fact that we spoil our dogs, and we spoil them with things.

If you're serious about a greener lifestyle for your dog, it's time to take stock of what's in your pooch's wardrobe and toy box, and make some valuable and long-lasting decisions about what he really needs.

PET SPENDING TRENDS

The APPMA tracks trends related to how people care for their pets. Their **2008 Pet Products Trend Report** included the following: "Lap of Luxury: High-end items to spoil companion animals are must-haves for pet owners that spare no expense to please their furry, feathered, and finned best friends. Items include faux mink coats for cold weather outings, feathered French day beds for afternoon naps, designer bird cages, botanical fragrances, and to top it all off, a rhinestone tiara!"

Items Your Dog Shouldn't Be Without

Even those lucky dogs who live as close to a *natural* existence as possible, with room to roam safely during the day, and a family that strives to keep them as physically sound as possible by providing exercise, a quality diet, comprehensive preventive care, and the necessary veterinary care—even those lucky dogs can't live without the following items:

- Food dish
- Water dish
- Collar
- Leash
- Identification tag
- Grooming essentials: brush, flea comb, toenail clippers, and toothpaste that's appropriate for dogs
- Dog bed
- Chew toys to relieve boredom
- Some kind of confinement system

If you were looking for the rhinestone tiara on this list…well, I know we all give in to temptation now and then…we can't help it. But the idea is to try to green your spending priorities. If you really want to indulge in a tiara for your diva dog, how about making one from recycled flea-market junk jewelry?

A Question of Quality

The next step in considering the impact of these necessary items on the environment is to look at the overall quality of the products—what they're made from, how they're made, where they come from, and what their life expectancy might be. You've already read about grooming products on pages 38 to 40. Now let's take a closer look at the other essentials.

Food and Water Dishes

Every dog in your family should have his own dish for food. Dogs can share a water dish. Lest you fear that your eco-friendly options in this department are going to limit you to stainless steel, take heart! Crockery is one of the best options for a food or water dish, and there are hundreds of sizes and styles available. Food and water dishes run the range from purely practical stainless steel and plastic in all colors and sizes to crockery in so many styles that finding one to fit your décor is very easy. You can also find nice bowls at thrift stores and yard sales.

Stainless steel bowls. These may not be elegant, whimsical, or even color-coordinated, but they have a few things going for them that make them very earth-friendly. The first is that they are durable. You'd have to throw or drop one with great force onto something hard to even ding one that's well made. Another is that they are easy to clean. With their non-porous surfaces, they won't trap and harbor bacteria. One

thing they are, though, is slippery when they're on a smooth surface. That's why they often come with non-slip rubber liners. While the rubber isn't an earth-friendly ingredient, it's a small strip that is valuable for the job it does. If your dog takes an interest in the rubber and wants to chew it, you should switch to a stainless steel bowl that can be put into a platform for food and water dishes, or you can use crockery instead.

Crockery bowls. The shapes and sizes that these glazed and baked earthenware bowls come in are quite varied—from fine china that resembles something that would grace the table of an elegant dinner party to a heavy, plain bowl best suited to the needs of a large dog who eats with gusto. Be sure the bowls you're interested in are coated with lead-free glazes designed to withstand temperature extremes so they won't leach or crack.

ONE SIZE DOES NOT FIT ALL

Before making a selection based on looks alone, consider the size and eating style of your dog. Be sure the bowl is heavy enough that it won't be pushed around by a large, boisterous eater. Be sure the sides are steep enough to keep the food securely in the dish, but not so steep that the dog needs to put his whole face in the bowl to get to the food at the bottom. Be sure there's enough surface area on the bottom of the bowl so your dog can comfortably eat from it.

Plastic bowls. Food or water bowls made from plastic are best avoided. They can seem like a fairly durable and economic alternative to stainless steel or crockery, but their downsides are discouraging. First, the toxic chemicals with which the plastic itself was made can leach into the food or water. Certainly the amounts in one or two servings won't cause significant ill health, but over time these undesirables can contribute to poor health and may exacerbate other conditions. Plastic is something a lot of dogs like to chew on, and you don't want your dog gnawing on the bowl. Large pieces, if swallowed, could cause internal damage.

WHERE ARE BOWLS MADE?

Christine Maller of Green Dog Pet Supply and John Mancinelli, a longtime employee of Earth Animal, concur: Most stainless steel bowls are imported from India. Most plastics are manufactured in China. Christine and John both keep a supply of locally crafted crockery bowls in their stores.

KEEP 'EM CLEAN

Be sure to wash your dog's food bowls after every meal so that by the next mealtime the bowl is clean and ready. As for water bowls, don't waste by overfilling them, but be sure there is fresh water in them throughout the day. You can recycle day-old drinking water by warming it up in the microwave and using it to moisten your dog's dry food.

Collars, Leashes, and Identification Tags

For years I used two cotton leashes to walk generations of dogs. I can't even remember where I originally got them. When one of them finally frayed and broke, I went to my local pet supply store to get a replacement, but there wasn't one like it. The only cotton leads they carried were 8- and 12-foot-long (2.4 and 3.7 meter) training leads. All the other leashes were made of leather or nylon. I shopped around, but no stores carried cotton leashes. I didn't want a leather leash (too heavy), so I bought a nylon one. I hate it. It's hard. It's slippery. And it's uncomfortable in my hand.

I've been resorting to an old leather leash I had buried away, but since doing the research for this book, I've learned where I can order what I want—at last! There's a line of organic cotton collars and leashes called Ruffin' It, made by Westminster Pets, that is produced in the United States with organic cotton from Africa and low-salt, earth-friendly dyes. A percentage of the sales of the products are donated to FORGE, a U.S.-based nonprofit organization that helps African communities to become more self-sufficient. Check them out at westminsterpet.com.

The collar and leash that your dog sport day in and day out can say a lot about his (or your) personality. Manufacturers have tapped into this and now offer an ever-increasing selection. But going green means avoiding unnecessary products that merely satisfy your impulse to buy a doggie whatnot. Rather than purchase a different dog collar to match your personal hobbies or fashion passions, consider buying inexpensive fabric with, say, a seashell pattern on it, and creating a simple bandana for your dog to wear when you go on your beach vacation. You can find fabric remnants of all kinds at thrift stores, and it's easy to recycle a cotton dress or blouse from a flea market into a bandana, too.

Of course there's nothing more classic (and often nothing that lasts longer) than a beautiful leather collar, but for some folks that's simply too plain, and for others, buying leather products is something to avoid altogether. And where is that leather from, anyway? The bulk of leather items are made from cattle hide, a by-product of the meat industry. The hides are treated in various ways and with different kinds of chemicals to produce the type of leather necessary for a particular item. Further chemical treatment can include dying the leather to turn it a particular color.

The most eco-friendly collars and leashes are those made with organic cotton or hemp. Hemp is super-strong. Most collars made from it are fashioned like the macramé bracelets that were popular in the 1970s, and give a truly eco-look to the dogs who wear them.

TAG ALONG

You probably know about the permanent ways to identify your pet: tattoos and microchips. While these can provide an extra level of protection should your dog become lost or stolen, neither can replace the tried-and-true identification tag a dog should wear on her collar at all times. This is the first thing people look for when they find a stray dog. The tag should include your dog's name and your phone numbers (home and cell). There's a great green choice out there, too: Tuff Tagz (tufftagz.com). These tags are made from hand-cut recycled aluminum, stamped and personalized, then buffed to a high shine for clear visibility.

GREENING THE HALLOWEENING

You're in good company if you like to dress up your canine companion for what is becoming one of the most popular holidays on the calendar, Halloween. This year, don't buy—redo! It's simple to make Princess a costume from one of your daughter's old ballet outfits, for example, or pimp up an old hooded sweatshirt with fabric paint and a pair of glue-on plastic sunglasses. Be creative—and be proud to show off your dog in a recycled outfit.

Beds That Can't Be Beat

Even if your bed is your dog's preferred place to snooze—or maybe because it is—a dog needs a dog bed of his own in your home. There are hundreds of beds to choose from. For an in-depth discussion about beds and bedding, see page 81. In the meantime, ask yourself the following three questions when it's time to invest in one:

1. Is the filling made from recycled materials? This should be clearly stated by the manufacturer.
2. What is the cover made from?
3. Where was the bed manufactured?

Toys to Last

More and more manufacturers are making toys from organic materials—especially cotton and hemp—and using natural rather than chemical dyes. These are definitely steps in the right direction. While plush toys come in the most adorable forms—from lifelike ducks to silly clown faces; rabbits, dinosaurs, and lizards; and even rings and circles—before splurging on one, consider how long the toy might last. Some dogs have what is called a "soft mouth" and enjoy holding and carrying a soft toy around. Others want to mangle them immediately, and still others will nibble away at their extremities or attachments, plucking off the plastic eyes or gnawing on the sewn toes. For the first kind of dog, plush may be the perfect toy. For the latter two types of dog, a more durable toy is probably a better choice.

NO MORE MISFITS

Remember the Island of Misfit Toys in the cartoon classic, **Rudolph the Red-Nosed Reindeer**? All the slightly broken toys wonder why no child wants them. There are many such toys in every neighborhood these days, and some are just waiting for a dog to love them. If you have a dog that enjoys carrying around and cuddling plush toys, look for stuffed animals at yard sales. Other dog-friendly yard-sale finds include balls, Frisbees, tennis rackets that you can use to hit balls farther away for a better chase, water toys for dogs that like to swim, and so on. A note of caution: be sure the item is safe for your dog. If you're not sure, supervise him when he's playing with it.

Caution: Plastic

Plastic toys, both hard and soft, also come in multiple forms. While word is getting out about the dangers to children of some of these plastics—and the plasticizers that are used to keep them flexible—there had been no significant studies on the effects on dogs and other pets until just recently. One thing we canine keepers know, though, is that dogs explore with their mouths, and puppies especially so. If there is concern about a small child sucking on these plastics, it would seem logical that there should be concern about puppies and dogs chewing on them.

The Phthalate Information Center at phthalates.org disputes the current concerns, but a May 2008 study done by the not-for-profit Environmental Working Group in Washington, DC, has demonstrated otherwise. Relative to plastics, it reports, "Dogs were contaminated with breakdown products of four plastic softeners (phthalates) at average levels higher than those in more than 80 percent of Americans tested nationally, at levels ranging between 1.1 and 4.5 times the average concentrations in people. These included breakdown products of DEHP, DBP, and DBzP, which are used in veterinary medicines, plastic containers and toys, shampoos, and a huge range of other consumer products. Six of seven phthalate breakdown products were found in dogs altogether. These chemicals pose risks for reproductive damage, birth defects, and cancer." The report is mandatory reading for anyone interested in this and the effects of other chemicals on dogs (and cats). Find it at ewg.org/reports/pets.

Rubber is a substance that many dogs enjoy chewing. Until recently, most of the rubber pet toys were made from synthetic rubbers, which contain petroleum products. Rubber is actually a naturally occurring substance, and more and more manufacturers are switching from synthetic to natural rubber for their products. Another option is a material called Zogoflex from West Paw Design. It's guaranteed tough and nontoxic, and is extremely durable—as well as available in a line of interesting shapes and colors. Check out the line at westpawdesign.com. Other environmentally conscious supply stores such as Green Dog Pet Supply and Earth Animal can advise you on strong yet safe chews, too. (See Resources on page 166 for the stores' contact information.)

Confinement for Safety and Seclusion

It's hard to look at a dog in a crate and not make the association that he's in a cage, trapped, and lonely. The truth is that when it is properly used, a crate can be a dog's very favorite place—the den where he can cuddle up and rest peacefully. For canine caretakers, being able to crate a dog makes car travel safer and easier, provides less confusion and worry during parties when a dog may tend to get underfoot, offers a great place to put a dog when a child who is afraid (or is too rough) is nearby, and comes in handy at other times when it's best for your dog to be properly confined.

Another purpose of a crate is to assist in housetraining. Because most dogs don't want to urinate or defecate where they sleep, they will hold it while in the crate and then want to be taken outside afterwards.

Both of these desirable uses for crates are only successful when the crate is properly used and the dog is properly trained to accept it as a great spot. It's easy to abuse the crate, though, by leaving a dog confined for way too long, by using it as a place to punish a dog, or by not understanding a puppy's bathroom needs, which are frequent. For many, a crate may be too large to fit in a small kitchen or mud room, making it impractical and therefore less likely to be used. This is when a confinement system can (and should) be utilized to serve the same purposes.

As with all accessories for dogs, there are many options. Crates are made of metal, plastic, and even collapsible nylon. Picking the one that's best suited for your dog and your home is a decision that's best made with the help of a trusted pet supply store associate or another professional who's familiar with your breed or type of dog. The greenest option is the one that's going to do its job for the longest time, and that could even be passed on to

your next dog or to someone else's dog when yours may no longer need it. Durability is key!

As for a confinement system, a baby gate works well when placed across the passageway from an all-purpose room such as a kitchen, wash room, or mud room. The gate you choose will depend on the size of your dog (as an adult), whether you mind stepping over the gate or want to be able to swing it open and closed, and what material it's made of. Again, the greenest option is the one that will last!

Items Your Dog Could Do Without

You may rightfully argue that some of the accessories on the list that follows are, in fact, things your dog can't live without. The one who is ultimately responsible for your dog's care and comfort is you, and the decision about what she needs is yours. As you learned in the other chapters in this book, it's not necessary to make the leap to a 100-percent green way of life overnight, but it's important to continually think about our consumption choices relative to their overall impact on the planet.

As you review this list, consider each of the items individually and collectively. If you use any of them, think about how you might reuse them. Can you recycle items once you're finished with them? And, ultimately, can you reduce or eliminate your need for them? Another thing to consider is whether you can craft substitutes using things you may already have at home. Some of the items and areas to consider are as follows:

Apparel. Bandanas, scarves, boots, coats, hats, hoodies, jackets, doggy jewelry, sunglasses or other eyewear, sweaters, etc. If you love dressing up your dog, look around your home for what you can reuse. If you're truly committed to reducing your consumption for the betterment of the planet, though, this is a habit you should seriously consider breaking. If you're using apparel for protection from the elements, that's a different matter. The health of your dog should come first.

Multiple beds. One or two beds (for upstairs and downstairs, or in the crate and outside the crate) are fine, but honestly, does your dog need more than that? If you're going to be somewhere for an extended but temporary amount of time (visiting relatives, for example), bring one of the existing beds along.

Multiple covers for beds. Quality dog beds come with removable liners that you can wash. Rather than purchasing additional liners, use an old blanket or sheet to cover a bed while you're washing the liner. When a liner gets worn out, then purchase another one—this is a good time to switch to organic cotton or bamboo fabric instead of a synthetic material.

Grooming supplies. Of course you want your dog to look good, and this can be accomplished with a few basics, plus your time and energy. Sure, the disposable towels or coat wipes seem convenient, but if you're serious about greener care, ditch them and use old towels or other rags that can be washed and reused. As for potions to clean eyes or ears, try all-natural remedies that can probably be concocted from ingredients you have in your pantry, or explore using herbal remedies from local sources. The resources in the back of this book (see page 166) are a good place to start.

Car seat covers. Be honest with yourself: Wouldn't an old blanket or sheet do just as well? It may not tuck in as nicely as something that's supposed to be custom fitted, but if your dog slobbers on or muddies it up, you won't feel as bad—and what a great way to recycle linens!

Toys. Dogs do like variety, but they also tend to like a particular kind of toy (or not). Once you understand what kinds of toys make your dog happy, choose super-tough items made from organic fabrics and recycled materials, or fashion them from items you have in the house.

Your Green Dog Accessory-Downsizing Action Plan

I know it's asking a lot to compromise where your decorating and pampering instincts are concerned, but compromise you must if your dog is truly going to live a greener lifestyle. Remember, you don't have to go cold turkey—or tofurky. Downsizing can be a gradual process. The cliché that change is hard is a time-tested one for a reason: it's true! But there's no excuse for not starting to change right now. This list will help.

LEVEL 1

You're taking this chapter to heart and noticing what kinds of supplies and gizmos you buy for your dog. You're asking yourself if they're really necessary. That's great! Keep questioning your need—for the things you have and the things you're tempted to acquire. Instead of buying a new dog toy, go home and play for an extra hour with your dog!

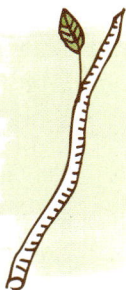

LEVEL 2

Three simple things you can do to fulfill this level are:

1. Buy a new toy only when an old toy is no longer useful or safe—and replace it with a more durable, eco-friendly alternative.
2. Walk past the aisle in your pet supply store where all the cute outfits are, and do not log on to your favorite doggy designer websites!
3. Find a place to take any plastic feeding or water dishes to be recycled, and replace them with locally crafted crockery or very durable stainless steel.

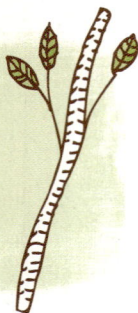

LEVEL 3

Your pup is living with just the necessities outlined in this chapter. Here are two suggestions:

1. When you think you need something new for your dog, think twice. If it's something that will last a long time and is necessary for his health or safety—and good mental health is part of this picture—then make an informed and satisfying purchase. For anything else, give yourself more time to consider whether what you're interested in is both necessary and made of the most eco-friendly materials.

2. Donate excess dog supplies that are still in good shape to your local animal shelter. Even that once just-had-to-have-it rhinestone tiara might make a fun item that could help a small dog appear more adoptable; perhaps the shelter could host a Fashion Adoption Day, where the dogs all sport something fun.

LEVEL 4

For those for whom Levels 1, 2, and 3 are easily managed, go ahead and implement the following changes:

1. Get rid of any plastic toys and accessories you think may be harmful to your pooch. Don't wait for a study like that done by the Environmental Working Group to confirm what you suspect may be harming your dog. This goes for items and products all over your home.

2. Talk to your local pet supply store managers about what kinds of things you'd like to see in their stores. Put together a list of eco-friendly items that they could recommend for caretakers of dogs of all ages, from puppies and active younger dogs to seniors.

3. Inspire others to make their own dog accessories. It's easy to craft bed covers from worn-out jeans, toys from solo socks, or sweaters from items your kids have outgrown.

CHAPTER

7

Greener
Getaways
WITH YOUR
Dog

IN THIS CHAPTER YOU'LL LEARN

What it means to travel green

How to cope when life takes you and
your dog beyond local

How to be green in other places

GREEN LIVING—FOR YOUR DOG AND YOU—ISN'T SOMETHING YOU DO FOR AN HOUR A DAY AND THEN FORGET ABOUT. Instead, it's something you practice continuously as it becomes less of a life-changing influence and more of a lifestyle pattern. Choosing to live in earth-friendlier ways at home, at your office, and in the ways that you shop shouldn't stop when you leave your part of the world. In fact, just as a guest is respectful of a host's hospitality, so travelers should be respectful of the places being visited because others call those places home. This means being mindful of your waste and your consumption, as well as your impact on property and people. It makes sense to incorporate the fundamentals of your green lifestyle while you and your dog are on the road.

Green Travel Principles

There are short trips (meeting up with a friend and her dog in a nearby park, for example) and long trips (drives to visit family or friends for holidays). Each trip you take with your dog has its own parameters relative to its eco-impact, and these are what you need to consider when preparing for them. When you make a commitment to traveling green, you continue your commitment to *reduce*, *reuse*, and *recycle*.

Most trips involve one or more of the following:

- Transportation
- Lodging
- Food and water
- Stuff (everything you bring along, such as leashes, bowls, poop bags—oh, and your stuff, too!).

Transportation

Whether you're going to travel near or far, you have to get there. Traveling with your dog means additional transportation considerations—and additional ways to practice greener living.

One of the greatest, simplest, and most earth-friendly ways to go places and get around with your dog is to take the shoe-leather express: walk! You should be doing this several times a day, anyway, for the physical and mental well-being of your canine companion. That said, there are certainly many more places you will want to go with your dog that are beyond a comfortable and safe walking distance, so what is the greenest way to go?

Depending on how often you use the car to take your dog to a nearby park or recreation area, consider reducing the frequency of your trips and extending the walk itself instead. While you may not be able to give your dog the off-leash time he'd get in the park, both of you will benefit from the longer walks. You'll get to know your neighborhood better this way, too.

WHY YOU **SHOULDN'T** BIKE

People have trained dogs to accompany them on bicycles for many years, and before the days of doggy treadmills, bicycling was one of the ways trainers kept show dogs and working dogs in peak condition. Seems like a great and green option, doesn't it?

The thing about biking with a dog is that a lot can go wrong. For this practice to be done properly, you need to have the right kind of harness for your dog and attach it properly to the bike. Then, your dog has to adjust to this contraption and accept it. Moreover, if you're cycling along and your dog spots a squirrel or another dog and decides to give chase, he could yank you hard enough that you could easily lose your balance, swerve, and crash. For all these reasons, biking is not a practical and safe option for getting you and your dog to different places without incident. If your destination is close by, walk; if distance is involved, consider driving, but reduce pup's carbon paw print with the ideas that follow.

Dogs and Cars

Whenever my in-laws come to my house with their dog Sadie, I am reminded of how much easier it is to be mobile with a single small dog. Sadie is a mixed breed that weighs about 20 pounds (9.1 kilograms). She has a seat of her own in the car, where she perches, safely strapped in, and watches the world go by. She loves riding in the car. She's well behaved, socialized, clean, and tidy, and goes everywhere with her family.

My two Dalmatians, on the other hand, take up an entire section of the car, necessitating that at least one of our vehicles be large enough to fit them—and two children, and me and my husband, of course. For them to be comfortable and safe, we need a dog bed in the back, as well as a protective divider to keep them from landing in our laps if I have to slam on the brakes. No matter how much we'd like a more eco-friendly hybrid or electric car, the ones currently on the market are simply out of the range of possibility as a family vehicle.

Certainly there are other options, and when our paid-for vehicle finally logs its last miles, there will be even more earth-friendly options to accommodate us. We can't wait.

In the meantime, we drive around feeling guilty about our emissions and our sheer dependence on driving. Thankfully, there's terrapass.com, a website devoted to educating and helping folks like us understand, reduce, and offset our carbon emissions (at least there's something we can do about emissions!). There, you can calculate the carbon emissions generated by your car, based on the kind of vehicle it is and the number of miles you drive in a year. Then you can purchase a carbon offset to fund clean energy and efficiency projects. It's all there on the site, so take a look, make a difference, and feel a little less guilty. Keep in mind that buying offsets is a trend. As such, a lot of companies are jumping on the bandwagon. Do your research on the company you want to buy the offsets from so you know your money is being spent in the ways they claim.

There are other aspects of using a car to transport your dog that can be evaluated for greater eco-friendliness. For instance, you might bring your dog along because she loves to ride in the car and you need to go pick up your kids from their after-school activities. If you didn't bring the dog, you might choose the more fuel-friendly car in the driveway, but instead you take the gas-guzzler because it's Rover-friendly. Hmm…what to do? That's right…leave Smoochie at home, and when you and the kids return, all of you go for a long walk with your precious pooch.

When you pack for yourself, your family, and your dog to go on a trip in the car, what do you bring? Remember *reduce, reuse, recycle*. If you're going where your dog will swim or play in the mud, keep some old towels in a mesh bag so they can be washed and reused for the next trip. (No paper towels.) If your dog will need water, fill some empty gallon containers, put them in a cooler, and bring along his water dish—for short trips there's no need for a collapsing bowl or portable drinking contraption. Longer trips may make them practical.

SNACKING ON THE ROAD

For many of us, a road trip hasn't officially started until we load up on drinks and snacks at the gas station or go through the drive-thru of a fast-food joint. Such indulgences can make an ordinary outing more fun and special, but if you're serious about greening your life, ask yourself if this stuff is really necessary. It takes more forethought and planning, but it's possible to make a road trip special and fun for all—even the dogs—with things you bring from home. For them, make sandwiches out of dog treats by putting organic peanut butter between two all-natural dog biscuits. For you, bring water or natural fruit juices in reusable containers for the human passengers. Bring your coffee, made just to your liking, in a reusable car mug—it has the added bonus of keeping your joe warm longer, too. Resist the protests of your children; they'll adjust. And as for your dog, the best treat of all is being with you.

Dogs and Airplanes

It's a means of travel for some top show dogs, but putting your dog on an airplane—especially if she's going to travel in the cargo area—should only be considered when no other safe options exist for traveling a long distance with your dog. That said, there may come a time when it's necessary for you to put your dog on a plane. Be sure to do plenty of research on the airlines themselves and their pet policies, as well as the kinds of carriers that are available for dogs traveling by air. Your primary considerations are the safety of your dog in his carrier and the handling he will receive from the airline itself. Like driving, flying is a modern convenience that is difficult, if not impossible, to live without. And like driving, flying contributes to global warming. At terrapass.com you can also offset your flying miles.

Dogs and Lodging

For those who remember sneaking a dog into hotels and bed-and-breakfasts: while it was fun, it was also scary to think you might be discovered and asked to leave. Fortunately there are now many lodging choices for those traveling with their four-footed friends. In fact, even high-end hotels such as the InterContinental not only welcome travelers' dogs, but woo them with things like "doggy goody bags." The InterContinental's Indigo hotel in Atlanta, Georgia, has a canine cocktail hour at which a portion of the sales of an Indigo martini (for people) goes to supporting a local dog park. That's progress!

PET-FRIENDLY PLACES

Finding lodging that accepts dogs is easier than ever; in fact, chances are that some of your favorite places to stay have pet policies in place. Ask at the desk. A great place to start your search online is through petswelcome.com. The site has been assisting travelers for more than a decade and has listings for chains, bed-and-breakfasts, ski resorts, cabins, support services such as pet sitters, pet-friendly places to visit, and much more.

Other green factors to keep in mind when you stay in hotels include:

- Be conscientious about water use, including ice for the room. To prevent possible infection from the hotel's water, provide home-bottled water for your dog to drink.

- Bring an old blanket from home for your dog. If he's going to sleep on the bed with you, it will not only protect the hotel's bedspread, but also provide a layer of protection between your dog and whatever chemicals are used to treat the spread for dirt and stains.

- Bring some old towels from home for your dog so you don't have to get hotel towels dirty. Old towels are softer and easier to use on your dog, anyway.

- Turn the lights, TV, radio, and your computer off when you won't be in the room. If you're concerned about leaving your dog alone in the room with no lights or "white noise," bring a nightlight and, of course, a favorite toy—the things you'd leave him alone with at home.

ARE YOU A GEOTOURIST?

A recent report entitled "Geotourism: The New Trend in Travel," prepared by the Travel Industry Association of America (tia.org) and sponsored by **National Geographic Traveler** explained that today's traveler "craves and expects authentic experiences. They want to return from a trip renewed or changed in some way." The study also reported that nearly one of every two travelers prefers to experience the local culture and support local businesses and their destinations. Tourism that sustains or enhances the geographical character of the place being visited — including its culture and environment — has been coined "geotourism". The TIA study showed that becoming a geotourist can be as simple as seeking out travel companies that make protecting and preserving the environment one of their goals, or supporting companies that make energy efficiency one of their everyday practices. Paying closer attention to hotels that ask guests to reuse towels, participating in recycling programs, and using energy-efficient heating and air conditioning are all examples of programs that are striving to reach the same goal of preserving the environment.

If this is a trend in tourism in general, certainly there's room for including your canine companion. Check into the possibility of bringing your dog along, and assure the organizers or proprietors that you're eco-conscious when it comes to caring for your best friend.

Food on the Road

One of the joys of traveling is trying new foods—even if it's at a diner that's famous for its apple pancakes. But when it comes to your dog's meals on the road, it's best to stick to the at-home menu. Be sure to bring along plenty of what she normally eats. If you cook for her, make meals ahead of time and freeze them into servings that are actually a bit smaller than normal. If you feed your dog kibble with or without canned food or other supplements, pack the same brands. If you offer your dog a raw diet, plan ahead and pack what you'll need in a cooler: fresh, organic ingredients in the right proportions aren't always available—or convenient.

Broken Habits

Dogs are creatures of habit and are most content when they follow a routine. Traveling is a sure way to upset this. Even if your dog is a frequent traveler, he may not adjust to the changes in your schedule as easily as you. When mealtimes don't come when expected or when food is offered in a strange place, he may lose his appetite. Don't be too concerned about missed meals, but be sure that your dog is drinking plenty of water. Consider flavoring the water with some low-fat, low-sodium chicken broth for extra palatability. If you'll be snacking while driving, bring along some healthy and easy-to-digest dog snacks such as organic biscuits, baby carrots, or steamed chicken cut up into bite-sized pieces.

Water, Water Everywhere

Nervous or excited dogs get thirsty and might not be too picky about their sources of water while on the road. This could include toilet bowls, puddles, other dogs' bowls, or streams. Certainly you don't want your dog drinking out of toilet bowls in hotels or others' homes—they may have been cleaned with harsh chemicals. And even the most pristine streams can carry giardia or other

microscopic organisms that can play havoc on your dog's digestive system. Traveling with plenty of water from your home can be a hassle, but it can save you a lot of heartache (and clean up) on the road. Fill recycled gallon jugs with cold water from your kitchen sink and store them in a cooler.

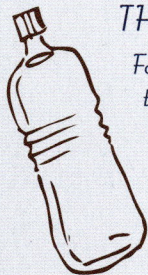

THE LONG AND WINDING ROAD

For long trips that will necessitate more water than it's practical to travel with, seek out sterilized water in gallon jugs or Willard Water (available in health food stores). Both of these sources are guaranteed sterilized, at least. When the water is gone, recycle the containers; I have a friend who cuts the bottoms and tops off of plastic gallon jugs and uses them to protect young, growing plants in his garden!

Stuff

Once upon a time it was called "looting" and "pillaging." Today it's called "shopping"—that's how primal the instinct is to take something from an unfamiliar place and make it part of your world. Today there are few destination locations that don't have gift shops or souvenir stands from which we can pillage for a price so that we return home with a piece of the place we visited.

For many of us, shopping is as important a part of traveling as seeing the sites, eating out, or luxuriating in a room we don't have to clean up. Small dogs may enjoy the attention they get while peering out of shoulder bags or tagging dutifully along as their guardians wander the aisles of shops, but they don't really care whether you buy anything. For bigger dogs that aren't allowed in stores, shopping is a complete yawn.

Travel Essentials

The greenest way to go when it comes to shopping while on vacation with your dog is to simply *reduce* (do without). Be sure to pack what you need for your dog before you leave home so that you have the following essentials:

- Collar or halter
- Leash
- Food and water dishes
- Food and water
- Bed
- Towels and old sheets for cleaning up or keeping clean

Knowing how fond people are of their dogs, more and more shopkeepers—especially those in touristy areas—are including products in their stores that are just for dogs. A lot of those products are really, really cute…or extravagant…or unique. A simple collar tag from another country is a small item that can remind you of a special place every time you see it on your dog. It's hard to pass up some of the fun and funky stuff we see for dogs in our travels. What to do?

Keep the mantra *reduce, reuse, recycle* in your head while you shop. Think about how the item is packaged. Consider the kind of store you're shopping in—is it one that supports greener living in some way, shape, or form? Is there such a store where you're going—one that showcases products made by local craftspeople, farmers, or bakers? Determine if the product will last; is it a quality item or a novelty? As in every other aspect of caring for your dog (and yourself, your family, your community, your country, your planet), making the best choice means making a conscious choice.

NO TAG, NO TRAVEL

One thing you want to be sure is securely in place and updated is your dog's identification tag. This small piece of metal (preferably made from a recycled object) could mean the difference between being reunited with your dog or losing her forever. You may have a backup identification system such as a tattoo or microchip for your dog, but nothing beats the immediate visibility and available information on a collar tag. The information that must be on the tag is your dog's name, your home phone number, and your cell phone number.

Your Green Dog Travel Action Plan

Traveling is about experiencing something new and different, and it's often about leaving the daily grind behind to live more leisurely. This is more challenging to do with a dog along, but can be enjoyable if you're prepared. Is it possible to travel green with your dog and still experience the indulgence of vacation time? I think so, and here are the levels at which you can make your efforts.

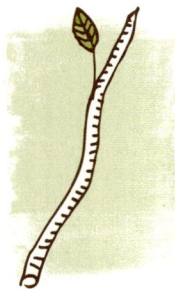

LEVEL 1

Regardless of how much you just want to get away from it all, you now look at the world through green-colored glasses and your carefree consumer side is shrinking...if it hasn't already wilted. Is it even possible to take your dog anywhere without being armed with biodegradable poop bags? If you've gotten this far in the book, I suspect not. This is where it all begins.

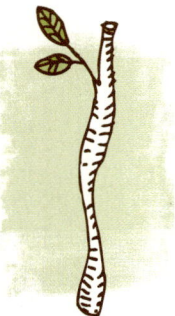

LEVEL 2

Some simple ways to achieve this level could include the following:

1. Find travel destinations that are closer to home, but equally intriguing. It's true that we often take fror granted what is nearest to us—like living in New York City and never going up the Empire State Building. What parks are near you that you have yet to explore?

2. Make an effort to find eco-friendly lodging where you can stay with your dog (see page 166). Chris Kingsley,

cofounder of petswelcome.com, says, "People who travel with dogs are savvy researchers—they need to be! So we see a definite connection between those who travel with pets and those who search out eco-friendly lodging." Chris encourages folks to ask about a particular place's contributions to greener living when they are doing their research. If you find something that petswelcome.com should add to its database, send him the information at chris@petswelcome.com.

3. Explore the listings of green hotels on economicallysound. com/green_living_on_the_road.html to find out if these places accept pets. If they don't, write a letter urging them to do so.

4. Ditch the disposables: paper towels, clean-up wipes, individual servings, etc. Replace these with things that can be reused, such as old towels and blankets, and the dog bowls from home.

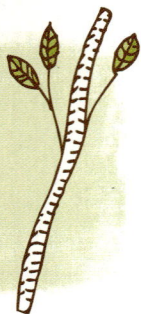

LEVEL 3

Another way to make a difference when you travel with your dog is to think about the kind of canine community you're visiting on your trip. Is it an area that's recently experienced some kind of hardship, such as hurricane damage or the loss of a large employer? How might you and your dog give back to a place you're visiting so that it's better for the people (and dogs) who live there? If your destination is a luxury hotel that allows dogs, notice what kinds of things the hotel provides for canine guests. Could they be greener? How? Can you help raise the staff's consciousness about what they provide for dogs (and people)?

LEVEL 4

You and your dog are bona fide geotourists, interested in helping to sustain the places you visit and traveling as greenly as possible. Here are four things you might do while you're out exploring:

1. Visit some local pet shops and take a look at their product lines. Do they include nontoxic, organic, eco-friendly products? If not, consider talking to the manager about some products you like to use and how they can make a big difference for the store's customers.

2. Log your miles if your trip requires you to travel any significant distance, and be sure to offset your carbon output when you get home (see page 141).

3. Plan eco-friendly outings with like-minded canine guardians, and spend some time after a group walk cleaning up the place you visit and brainstorming about ideas to get other dog people involved.

4. Whenever possible during your travels, buy local and organic. If you like to share your food with your dog (and let's face it, who doesn't?), you'll feel better, and so will she, when you're both savoring a slice of organic peach from the orchard down the road!

Deep Greening Your Dog

IN THIS CHAPTER YOU'LL LEARN

What to do to make the ultimate
green start

Ways to get green-centives

How to remember that today
is tomorrow

THROUGHOUT THIS BOOK I'VE STRESSED THAT TO MAKE A DIFFERENCE, YOU NEED ONLY START SLOWLY AND DO AS LITTLE OR AS MUCH AS YOU WANT. Options range from the simplest changes, such as choosing organic foods to serious lifestyle-change commitments such as incorporating more holistic dog healthcare practices or walking your dog more in your own neighborhood rather than driving to a park for exercise.

As you've seen from how the information is broken out in this book, there are distinct areas of your dog's life and environment that you can green. One by one, these changes intertwine and can make a big difference in reducing your dog's carbon paw print. You may want to keep a green dog log to track the green efforts you're taking on—and the progress you're making (including consequential changes to your dog's health, which may amaze you).

This chapter is a springboard for taking even greater action. On the personal level, it explores the greenest option for acquiring a dog. On community, country, and even global levels, it explores ways to make changes that affect a wider circle than that of your dog, your family, and your friends. And on a philosophical level, this chapter explores how to stay in a green mind-set.

The Ultimate Green Start

The idea I'm going to present now is so essentially green that treehugger.com has it as its top tip in the *How to Green Your Pet Guide,* which you can search for on the site. What is it? *Adopt from a shelter.*

Purebred Dogs

My career as a writer concerned with dog subjects started at the *American Kennel Gazette*, the official publication of the American Kennel Club (AKC), so it feels practically blasphemous for me to support treehugger on this. But it can't be denied: there are far too many dogs, including purebred dogs, in shelters. Under the umbrella of the AKC (which is technically a club of clubs), breeders and enthusiasts of the more than 150 recognized breeds spend the better part of their time touting the advantages of purebred dogs. They'll tell you the only way to have a dog that truly matches your lifestyle is to understand the traits of particular purebred dogs, and then pick the breed whose characteristics are best suited to the way you live. This makes sense and should be a consideration in choosing any dog.

But there's another side of the sport. People whose purebreds compete at dog shows, obedience trials, hunting tests and trials, herding events, lure-coursing events, and other specialty sports that showcase the finer points and abilities of those breeds are forever hoping to find just the right genetic combination to land them a standout. To do that, they breed their dogs. The dogs have many puppies, most of which are average, not extraordinary. The breeders keep the pups they think have the greatest potential, and they sell the others.

Breeding is an addictive pastime. When you acquire a puppy with great potential for the show ring or hunt field, or for keeping coyotes off your farm, you marvel at every step that pup takes toward the fulfillment of his destiny. When he's excelling at his job, how can you resist the urge to keep the line going or try to better it? If you aren't inclined to breed him, others around you

who would like their dogs to do as well as yours will encourage you to. And so the sport of dogs is perpetually fueled. In fact, the Westminster Kennel Club dog show, which takes place every February in New York City, is the longest-running continuous sporting event in the United States behind the Kentucky Derby. Safe to say—like thoroughbred racing—it's not going away.

Puppy Mills

But what about all those other puppies, the ones who weren't selected by the breeders as the cream of their crops? AKC registration statistics for 2007 tallied litter registrations at 392,334 and those of individual dogs at 812,452. A decade or so ago the AKC was registering more than a million dogs a year, so the number is dropping, and that's in large part due to a heightened awareness of the issues around breeding purebred dogs, including the percentage of pups that might be registered by indiscriminate breeders, who egregiously breed quantity over quality (often referred to as "puppy mill" breeders). The AKC has done a lot to put these kinds of breeders out of business—and continues to do so.

Still, more than 800,000 dogs is a lot of pups, and that's just the count in *one year*. And that's just the American Kennel Club; there are other purebred registries in the U.S. and around the world. And that's just the dogs that are actually registered; sometimes breeders (or new owners) forget to send in the paperwork to complete the registration process. You probably have a good idea about what's happening to those cast-off dogs.

SOBERING STATS

It's difficult to accurately assess the numbers of dogs and cats that enter shelters across the United States — or the percentage that are euthanized. The American Society for the Prevention of Cruelty to Animals (ASPCA) works with other humane groups to put together annual statistics on pet overpopulation and euthanasia. Check out the following, from their statistics for 2007:

- Approximately 5 to 7 million companion animals enter shelters across the United States every year.
- Approximately 3 to 4 million companion animals in shelters are euthanized due to lack of space or resources to adequately care for them (60 percent of dogs and 70 percent of cats).
- 25 percent of dogs who enter shelters are purebred.
- Less than 20 percent of the dogs who enter shelters are reunited with their owners.
- Only 10 percent of the animals received by shelters are spayed or neutered, whereas 75 percent of owned pets are spayed or neutered.

The Shelter Crisis

In addition to the sheer number of purebred puppies being born, there are other reasons why animal shelters are full of dogs. "Behavior issues are a top reason dogs end up in shelters," says David Frei, Director of Communications for the Westminster Kennel Club and a former board member of a shelter in Seattle, Washington. The dog is too wild, for example, or it barks excessively. Remember, though, that the relationship works both ways: the dog may have acted up because it was being mistreated, or the family may lack dog training skills or experience—things the family would not admit to the shelter. "Another reason," Frei continues, "is that the people go through a lifestyle change that doesn't accommodate the dog…like a divorce or an allergy or a move."

For Frei, who has spent the better part of his life in the world of purebred dogs and who is recognized by millions as the television host of the Westminster Kennel Club dog show, it's all about education when it concerns bringing a dog into one's life. "The absolute greenest thing to do," he says, "is to fully prepare yourself for what dog ownership is about, what it entails, what you want, and what you're getting yourself into. Fewer dogs would be in shelters," he claims, "if people were really prepared. They would either put off their decision to get a dog or they would acquire one they could truly commit to for the lifetime of the dog."

Frei feels that one thing those seeking canine companionship can count on if they've been thorough in their search for a purebred dog is predictability. "All puppies are cute," he says, "and all dogs are lovable in some way. But how do you know how big your puppy will get, or what kind of coat it will have, or whether there are any breed-specific medical conditions you should be aware of if you aren't sure of the dog's genetic background? Truly responsible breeders," he advises, "will stand behind their puppies and dogs, guaranteeing a look and a temperament, and helping owners in whatever way they can through the life of the dog."

Purebred Rescue

Not all breeders heartlessly or mindlessly loose litters of puppies upon the planet to meet what fate befalls them. They consider every puppy extra-special and make sure that their pups find "forever homes." They include language in their contracts stating that if the people who adopt their puppies are unable to care for them for any reason, they will take them back—no questions asked—just as David Frei pointed out.

These breeders feel that way, not only about their own pups, but also about the breed (or breeds) they are involved with. When they learn that there is a golden retriever in a nearby shelter, for instance, they will go get it, and either care for it themselves

until they can find a permanent home, or put the dog in a foster home. Such folks form the vast network of what is now known as purebred rescue. Like shelter workers, they are the guardian angels for many abandoned dogs.

If you're determined to share your life with a particular breed of dog—and there are many compelling reasons to want to do so—it's great to know that you don't need to track down a breeder and find a litter of puppies. It's easy and wonderful to acquire a dog through purebred rescue—and these dogs are available in all ages. The folks who foster the rescue dogs have lived with them in a home environment and are able to tell you a lot about the dogs' personalities and quirks. They know whether a dog is fully house-trained, whether she gets along with other dogs or children, whether she has a bad chewing habit, or how she has responded to particular medication. They have usually bonded with the dog in some capacity and want to ensure that she will never need another home again.

For this reason, these breed rescuers will be brutally honest with you about what the dog needs—and brutally honest about whether they think you can provide it. You may be rejected as the choice for a particular dog. If you are, don't take it personally. Understand that the rescuers truly have the best interest of the dog in mind; work with them to find a dog that is right for you. It will be well worth it.

All AKC breed clubs have a rescue component now, so you can start your search at the AKC website, akc.org. Then search for the breed you like, access its website, and find the link that takes you to the rescue coordinator. There are many rescues among the dogs listed on petfinder.com, and it's a very easy site to search for both a particular breed and a geographic location. You can also do a Google search for the breed + rescue (for example "Shih Tzu + rescue").

Rescues—whether they come from the foster homes of purebred rescue groups or the cages of local animal shelters—are dogs that need homes, and they provide the ultimate "recycling" opportunity for people who want a canine companion.

NEXT STEP: SPAY OR NEUTER

Shelter and rescue dogs are typically spayed or neutered before they're released to a new home. Why? So they won't perpetuate the overpopulation problem, of course. And it's best for the health of the dog, too. (For more information on this topic see page 43.) There's no reason why your dog should not be spayed or neutered. Certain medical research refutes the value of performing this procedure before puberty, but there's also research that supports it. Like the question of whether and how often to vaccinate your dog, you need to be informed, work with a trusted veterinarian, and make your decision in the best interest of your dog. But spay or neuter you **must**!

In Asheville, North Carolina, the Humane Alliance is dedicated to providing a non-lethal solution to the pet overpopulation problem, and one of the ways it does that is to provide high-volume, high-quality spay and neuter services. By offering an affordable option to people who couldn't otherwise afford to have their pets spayed or neutered, the Humane Alliance has been able to significantly reduce the number of homeless animals and consequently the number of euthanized pets. The organization also provides resources for other groups around the country interested in offering similar programs. Visit its website at humanealliance.org.

Green-centives

Key features of this book are the four levels of green action steps reviewed at the end of each chapter. Level 4 has stressed going beyond small, personal steps, and has provided tips and ideas for extending green dog-keeping into your community.

Along those lines, it's helpful to know that there are organizations out there that can keep you focused. They can provide you with additional tips, put you in touch with like-minded folks, and inspire you to keep on going when you feel like you've hit a wall. This section touches on some of those organizations. There are more and more of them being established every day; in fact, maybe yours will be the one that dog caregivers around the country—and even the world—will be turning to next.

Going to Green Fairs and Festivals

Don't you love finding a group of like-minded dog owners you can hang out with and "talk dogs"? For many people, such groups are formed at special parks where dogs are allowed to play off lead in protected areas. There, your dog has a great time sniffing and playing and doing doggy things, while you find out who feeds what, the favorite local vets, whether ticks are a problem in the area, and so on.

Green fairs and festivals are like dog parks for individuals and businesses that care about greener living. They are a way to bring everyone together in one place at one time so newcomers can sniff out their options and seasoned "greenies" can gain inspiration from new developments or ideas. Green Fairs are a great place to make contacts if you're thinking about using more sustainable materials in building projects, switching to solar or wind power, or even exploring nontoxic cleaning options.

Called "parties with a purpose," one of these, Green Festival, is a joint project of Global Exchange and Co-op America, two leading nonprofit organizations that have been dedicated to environmental and social justice for more than 25 years. Their site, greenfestivals.org, offers a forum for exploring and building sustainable solutions for communities and the environment, as well as a listing of its green festivals. Check out ecobusinesslinks.com/green_fairs_sustainable.htm for links to other green fairs around the United States and the world.

The Natural Resources Defense Council (NRDC), a United States environmental action group, launched an ancillary website called "It's Your Nature" where people can go to help put together green events for their communities. Visit itsyournature.org to find a lot of ideas.

Action Plan Assistance

When I stumbled on the tab announcing "Action!" at globalwarming101.com— part of the Will Steger Foundation—I was delighted to find a "Template for Action" frame that mirrors this book's four action levels. This frame offers six steps that can form the basis for an action plan for tracking global warming issues that relate to us dog guardians!

Here's a brief summary of the steps in the template, with some tips about adapting them for you and your green dog.

1. EDUCATE YOURSELF ABOUT GLOBAL WARMING.

   I hope this book has helped in this regard. But check out the site's reading list to learn a great deal more about this complex topic.

2. **BEGIN BY CHANGING YOURSELF.**

The second step in globalwarming101's "Template for Action" provides a link to "Carbon Neutral Strategies," but for the dog-lover in you these strategies are what this book is all about. Read them, make changes, and be inspired to make more.

3. **FIND OR ASSEMBLE A GROUP OF COMMITTED PEOPLE.**

For you, it may be your dog park's human visitors, your veterinarian's community, or pet store managers in your area. Talking to others is how you'll find out who is interested; when you've identified them, start holding meetings.

HELP FROM THE STEGER FOUNDATION

From the globalwarming101 website comes this advice, too: "Something to keep in mind when you're creating your goals and objectives is SMART decision-making. SMART stands for "Specific, Measurable, Achievable, Realistic, and Timely." You can begin with some pretty lofty goals (such as the desire to make your community 100 percent carbon neutral), but the goals have to be broken down into manageable activity chunks that have specific measures of success. "For example, rather than have a goal of "Get everyone in the community to use biodegradable bags," the SMART way of stating that goal would be to say, "Demonstrate the eco-advantages of biodegradable bags to people using the dog park in spring. Follow up with people throughout the summer."

4. **IDENTIFY YOUR COMMUNITY'S MOST PRESSING GLOBAL-WARMING-RELATED ISSUES AND NEEDS.**

The first step in your plan should be a needs assessment. Take a look around your canine community and think about ways to most effectively and easily tackle clear problems. For example, converting dog-park frequenters to using biodegradable bags or working with a major pet supply store to carry more eco-friendly dog products.

5. **IDENTIFY RESOURCES IN YOUR COMMUNITY.**

To be effective, your group needs to assess its resources for achieving certain goals. For instance, does anyone personally know any of the pet store managers? Can you determine your group's financial impact on the pet store? It's also a good idea to identify what might get in the way of achieving your group's goals. Perhaps the pet store won't order its supplies from anyone but a distributor on a national level. How will you address that obstacle?

6. **BUILD A STRATEGY TO REACH YOUR GOAL.**

Just as you do when you follow a map, you need to know what to expect between your starting and ending points, and how you will get "there." Make a list of all the steps you need to take to reach your goal within a certain time frame, and assign tasks to group members. Your meetings will involve reviewing what was accomplished, by whom, and when, as you work toward your goals. Why not conduct your meetings at the dog park so your dogs can participate, too?

Today Is Tomorrow

You may be thinking, "Wow, I don't have time for all this, even though I want to make my home and my world healthier for my dog and myself." That's why this chapter is ending with three simple words—the words that have followed you through the book, the words that are coming up more and more in societal discourse, the words that are elemental and essential for living a greener life: *reduce, reuse, recycle.*

Like rehearsing a business presentation or visualizing your way through a challenging encounter, repeating these three words to yourself as you go through your day will bring them to life. When they are part of your mind set, you won't be able to go into a pet store without thinking about products relative to the ingredients or materials used, their packaging, and whether it's wise to make a purchase at all. You'll start to realize you could simply make do with something you already have. You may feel passionate enough to decide that today's the day you talk to the manager about bringing in more eco-friendly selections. When you notice yourself thinking and acting this way, you'll be living a greener life. And if that's how you think today, imagine how you'll be thinking—and living—a year or two or 10 from now.

Resources

There is an abundant amount of information online about green living, and most of it is quite thought–provoking. Even if the catalyst for learning about this topic is your canine companion, I suspect you'll find yourself drawn into the subject more deeply the more you learn, and soon you'll be compelled to try to live in a greener way in all aspects of your life. As with most subjects, though—especially trendy and current ones—the amount of information on the Web is staggering (and growing daily).

Faced with information overload, I think the best strategy is to stay focused. The resources provided here are ones that I consider to be the best places to direct your attention—relative to your dog and you. The information on these sites is reliable, comprehensive, and targeted. That said, if you find any others that you think I would like to know about, please email me at Dominique.devito@gmail.com—I am very interested! I will also post and update this list on the publisher's website, www.larkbooks.com.

Green Lifestyle

www.treehugger.com This is a great site for everything green, from getting informed to taking action.

www.terrapass.com Describing itself as a site to "restore the balance," Terrapass has instant carbon-footprint calculators, information on ways to offset carbon emissions, and all sorts of energy-saving tips and products.

www.emagazine.com This is the online home of *E/The Environmental Magazine*, "the handbook for living lightly on the earth." True to the mission of its flagship magazine, the website helps people learn what they can do to make a difference relative to the environment.

http://grist.org Here you'll find environmental news and policy to keep you up to date on the issues.

http://planetgreen.discovery.com/tv/ At last, a 24-hour cable television program devoted to eco-lifestyles. And this is a very informative website, as well—a sister site of www.treehugger.com.

www.sundancechannel.com/thegreen This website is affiliated with the television station of the same name, which broadcasts a wide range of issues on the environment.

www.this-greenlife.com "A pet lover's perspective on living healthy and green" is its slogan.

www.lowimpactliving.com This site helps you figure out how to get started on and work through projects to make your home/living space more eco-friendly.

www.theworldwomenwant.com Women make or influence 85 percent of purchases in the United States. This website was created to give spending women green power, individually and collectively. Check it out!

www.biggreenpurse.com Shoppers are invited to pledge to make a difference by spending on eco-friendly products.

www.ecorazzi.com This site provides "the latest in green gossip." It has several categories to choose from when you're looking for interesting news about high-profile folks and their green efforts. Fun!

www.nativeenergy.com Its slogan is "bringing new renewables to market." Here you can calculate your carbon footprint and offset it with renewable energy credits, which support projects to make the world a greener place.

www.aromaweb.com On this site, you'll find a great deal of information about using aromatherapy as a complementary treatment, including profiles of the essential oils and what they can be used for.

Green Dog (or Pet)

www.earthdoggy.com Here's a site that features eco-friendly products.

www.greatgreenpet.com Earth-friendly pet supplies can be found here.

www.poopbags.com For ordering 100-percent biodegradable poop bags in a variety of sizes, try this.

www.doggyarchy.com "Eco-chic, healthy canine comfort" (hemp beds for dogs) are offered here.

www.thebrushbuddy.com Dave Fortson invented this eco-friendly brush-and-towel combination that allows dog owners to brush, clean, and groom their dogs after walks and outdoor adventures. It's made from 100-percent recycled rubber and packaging.

www.greendogpetsupply.com This is the website for Green Dog Pet Supply, a shop located in northeastern Portland, Oregon, that specializes in "environmentally friendly supplies and gifts for dogs, cats, and their people." The company's focus is on exceptional nutrition and sustainable products.

www.earthanimal.com The website for this store in Westport, Connecticut, offers natural, holistic, and organic products with environmental integrity, including food, treats, vitamin supplements, and herbal remedies for dogs, cats, and other pets.

Pet Food

www.stevesrealfood.com "Making real raw foods and nothing less since 1998." Also, all their boxes, and plastic and foil bags are recyclable.

www.wholepetfoods.com A "natural pet grocery store since 1998." Its motto: "A holistic, organic and natural means of pet nutrition is the foundation of a healthy, happy life for your animal companions." The site offers a wide variety of foods, treats, and supplements, as well as toys, bowls, beds, and more.

www.rawmeatybones.com This website provides information and resources on Dr. Tom Lonsdale's approach to feeding a raw diet.

www.wellpet.org "A forum for natural pet care." The purpose of Wellpet is to get people thinking and learning about what they feed their pets.

Pet Health

www.avma.org The American Veterinary Medical Association (AVMA) is an organization that represents more than 76,000 veterinarians in a variety of practices and services across the United States. If you want to find out what the veterinary profession's position is on something, you can start your search here. Established in 1863, AVMA "acts as a collective voice for its membership and profession."

www.ahvma.org The website of the American Holistic Veterinary Medical Association. Organized to "function as a forum for the exploration of alternative and complementary areas of health care in veterinary medicine," the AHVMA maintains a directory of holistic veterinarians that you can access on this site.

http://householdproducts.nlm.nih.gov/index.htm This online database of the United States Department of Health & Human Services lists the ingredients in common household products—everything from lawn-care products and cleaners to pet-care items and personal care products—and describes their possible health effects and how to handle the products safely.

www.animalchiropractic.org and **www.avcadoctors.com** Both these sites are run by the Animal Veterinary Chiropractors Association. This group, like the AVMA and AHVMA, holds an annual conference for its members and maintains a database of certified veterinary chiropractors in the United States and around the world.

www.altvetmed.org This website, Alternative Veterinary Medicine, was launched in January 1996 with the intent of providing sound, basic information on complementary and alternative therapies in veterinary medicine. Through it, you can access many articles relevant to particular illnesses or diseases.

www.ivas.org The website of The International Veterinary Acupuncture Society. Whether you want to find a certified veterinary acupuncturist anywhere in the world or study to be one, this is the site you need to search.

Pet Travel

www.petswelcome.com This is the Internet's largest pet/travel resource, with listings for the United States and Canada, including B&Bs, resorts, campgrounds, beaches, and more.

Pet Adoption

www.petfinder.com This amazing site has facilitated the adoption of 12 million pets since 1995. A great site to browse, it allows you to access shelters and rescue groups near you and to read about pets looking for homes.

Recommended Reading

There are so many great books about dogs and caring for them. The list that follows includes some of my personal favorites, as well as material that can assist in aspects of greener living, including books about advanced nutrition and alternative health care.

Bell, Kristen Leigh. *Holistic Aromatherapy for Animals: A Comprehensive Guide to the Use of Essential Oils and Hydrosols with Animals*. Forres, Scotland: Findhorn Press, 2002

Billinghurst, Ian. *The BARF Diet: Raw Feeding for Dogs & Cats Using Evolutionary Principles*. BARF World ed. Danville, CA: Ian Billinghurst, 2001

Brown, Kathleen. *10 Herbs for Happy, Healthy Dogs*. Storey Country Wisdom Bulletin, a-260. North Adams, MA: Storey Publishing, 2000

De Vito, Carlo. *10 Secrets My Dog Taught Me: Life Lessons from a Man's Best Friend*. Emmaus, PA: Rodale Books, 2005

Dunbar, Ian. *How to Teach a New Dog Old Tricks*. 3rd ed. Berkeley: James & Kenneth Publishers, 1996

Engel, Cindy. *Wild Health: Lessons in Natural Wellness from the Animal Kingdom*. New York: Houghton Mifflin, 2002

Flaim, Denise. *The Holistic Dog Book: Canine Care for the 21st Century*. With a foreword by Michael W. Fox. New York: Wiley Publishing, 2003

Goldstein, Martin. *The Nature of Animal Healing: The Definitive Holistic Medicine Guide to Caring for Your Dog and Cat*. New York: Ballantine, 2000

Goldstein, Susan and Robert Goldstein, VMD. *The Goldsteins' Wellness & Longevity Program: Natural Care for Dogs and Cats*. Neptune City, NJ: T.F.H. Publications, 2005

Graham, Helen and Gregory Vlamis. *Bach Flower Remedies for Animals*. Forres, Scotland: Findhorn Press, 1999

Hourdebaigt, Jean-Pierre. *Canine Massage: A Complete Reference Manual*. 2nd ed. Wenatchee, WA: Dogwise Publishing, 2004

Kaplan, Laurie. *Help Your Dog Fight Cancer: What Every Caretaker Should Know about Canine Cancer, Featuring Bullet's Survival Story*. 2nd ed. Briarcliff, NY: JanGen Press, 2008

Kerns, Nancy. *The Whole Dog Journal Handbook of Dog and Puppy Care and Training*. Guildford, CT: Lyons Press, 2007

Knapp, Caroline. *Pack of Two: The Intricate Bond Between People and Dogs*. New York: Dell Publishing (Delta), 1999

Kostigen, Thomas M. *You Are Here: Exposing the Vital Link Between What We Do and What That Does to Our Planet*. New York: HarperOne, 2008

MacDonald, Carina Beth. *Raw Dog Food: Make It Easy for You and Your Dog*. Wenatchee, WA: Dogwise Publishing, 2003

Martin, Ann N. *Food Pets Die For: Shocking Facts about Pet Food*. With a foreword by Shawn Messonier. 3rd ed. Troutdale, OR: NewSage Press, 2008

McConnell, Patricia. *For the Love of a Dog: Understanding Emotion in You and Your Best Friend*. New York: Ballantine Books, 2007

McConnell, Patricia. *The Other End of the Leash: Why We Do What We Do Around Dogs*. New York: Ballantine, 2003

Messonnier, Shawn. *Natural Health Bible for Dogs & Cats: Your A–Z Guide to Over 200 Conditions, Herbs, Vitamins, and Supplements*. Roseville, CA: Prima, 2001

O'Driscoll, Catherine M. *Shock to the System: The Facts About Animal Vaccination, Pet Food and How to Keep Your Pets Healthy*. Wenatchee, WA: Dogwise Publishing, 2006

Pryor, Karen. *Don't Shoot the Dog!: The New Art of Teaching and Training*. 3rd ed. Gloucestershire, United Kingdom: Ringpress Books, 2002

Schultze, Kymythy R. *Natural Nutrition for Dogs and Cats: The Ultimate Diet*. Carlsbad, CA: Hay House, 1999

Schwartz, Cheryl. *Four Paws, Five Directions: A Guide to Chinese Medicine for Cats and Dogs*. Berkeley: Celestial Arts, 1996

Smith, Cheryl S. *Dog Friendly Gardens, Garden Friendly Dogs*. Wenatchee, WA: Dogwise Publishing, 2004

Talley, Jessica Disbrow and Eric Talley. *The Organic Dog Biscuit Cookbook: Over 100 "Tail Wagging" Recipes from the Bubba Rose Biscuit Company*. Kennebunkport, ME: Cider Mill Press, 2008

Tellington-Jones, Linda and Sybil Taylor. *The Tellington TTouch: A Revolutionary Natural Method to Train and Care For Your Favorite Animal*. New York: Penguin Press, 1993

Index

Acupuncture, 49–50

Animal communicators, 50–51

Aromatherapy, 51

Attention, 37, 45

BARF, See Dog food

Carbon footprints, 9

Chiropractic treatment, 52

Cleaning products, 84–87

Confinement, 130–131

Diet, 37, 62

Dishes, 23, 122–124

Dog beds, 81-83, 88, 126–127

Dog food, 14–29, 146, 169

    Home-cooked diets, 25–26

    Raw-based diet, 19, 24–25

Dog goods, 120–135

Dog waste, 101–102, 110–117

    Biodegradable bags, 114

Essential oils, 51–52, 60

Exercise, 37, 41–43

Parasites, 57, 62

Feeding, See Dog food

Fleas, 32, 35, 57–58

Flower essences, 53–54

Garlic, 62

Green healthcare, 10

Grooming, 35, 38–41

Heartworms, 61

Health, 32–67

Holistic remedies, 33, 48–58

Homeopathy, 55

Home care, 71–89

Lodging, 143–145

Massage, 55–56

Mosquitoes, 61

Nutrition, 35, 37

Paws, 72

Preventative care, 37

Puppy mills, 158

Purebreds, 157

Shelters, 159–162

Spaying and neutering, 37, 43, 162

Stress, 37, 44

Supplements, 23

Ticks, 32, 35, 59–60

Toys, 127–129

Travel, 138–153

Treats, 20

TTouch, 55–56

Vaccinations, 35, 46–48

Veterinarians, 34–36

Water, 23, 146–147

Yard maintenance, 92–107

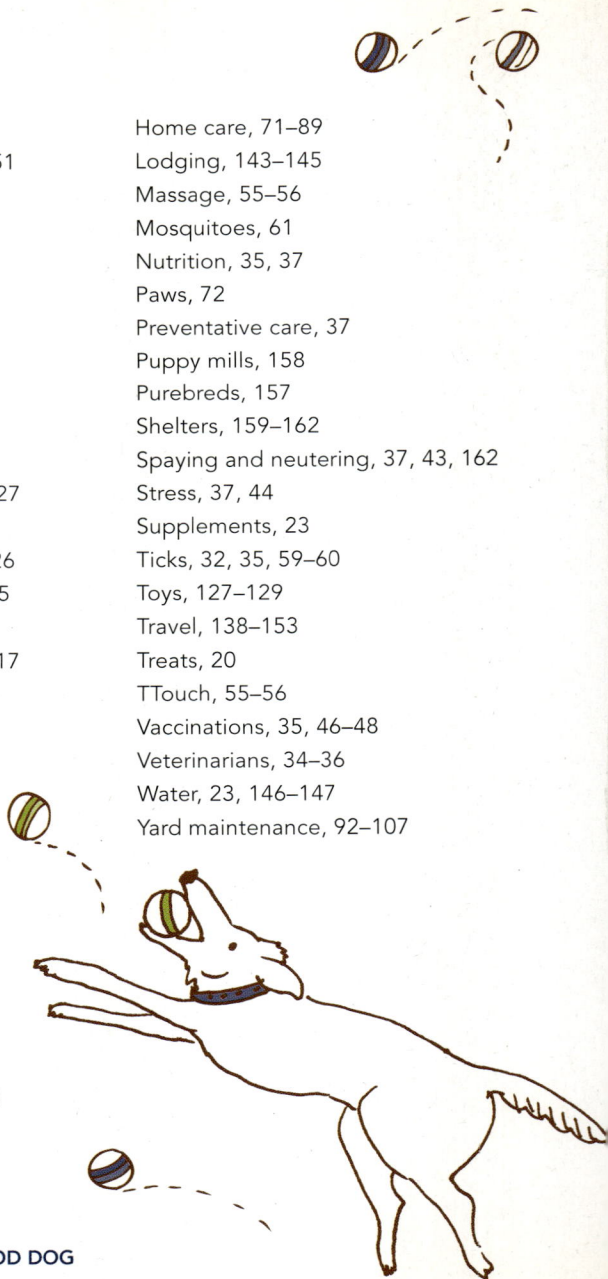